11-15-01

D0901661

MOTORCYCLE JOURNEYS THROUGH
NORTHERN MEXICO

Other Touring Guides in
The Motorcycle Journeys Series

Motorcycle Journeys Through New England

Motorcycle Journeys Through The Appalachians

Motorcycle Journeys Through The Southwest

Motorcycle Journeys Through The Alps and Corsica

Motorcycle Journeys Through Baja

Motorcycle Vagabonding In Japan

Also From Whitehorse Press

Motorcycle Touring and Travel:
A Handbook of Travel by Motorcycle
by Bill Stermer

MOTORCYCLE JOURNEYS THROUGH NORTHERN MEXICO

BY NEAL DAVIS

A Whirlaway Book
Whitehorse Press
North Conway, New Hampshire

Whitehorse Press books are also available at discounts
in bulk quantity for sales and promotional use. For
details about special sales or for a catalog of
motorcycling books and videos, write to the Publisher:
  Whitehorse Press
  P.O. Box 60
  North Conway, New Hampshire 03860-0060
  Phone: 603-356-6556 or 800-531-1133
  Fax: 603-356-6590
  E-mail: CustomerService@WhitehorsePress.com
  Web site: www.WhitehorsePress.com

ISBN 1-884313-20-5

5   4   3   2   1

Printed in the United States of America

This book is dedicated to all the wonderful Mexican people I have encountered while doing research for this book. My fumbling requests in broken Spanish for directions or information were almost always met with a smile and a willingness to offer whatever help they could provide. Mexico is a beautiful country and the people make it more so. *¡Gracias mis amigos!*

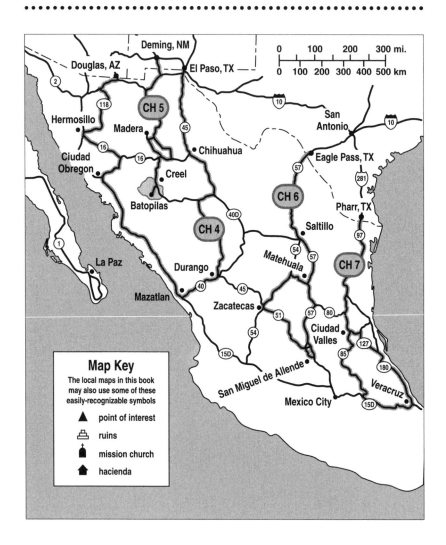

Map Key

The local maps in this book may also use some of these easily-recognizable symbols

▲ point of interest

⌂ ruins

🛐 mission church

🏠 hacienda

Contents

••

Foreword

When Dan Kennedy of Whitehorse Press proposed that I write a book about motorcycling in Mexico, my first thought was, "Why me?" What qualifications did I have to undertake such a proposal? It certainly wasn't a wealth of experience in formal writing. For many years, I have traveled roads throughout the U.S. and much of the rest of the world on bikes. I think it is the best way to meet locals, learn about where you are going, and get the "flavor" of an area. In so doing, I have grown to love Mexico and the Mexican people and have traveled there for more than 25 years. This country which adjoins the U.S. to the south has a rich history and culture, yet many never visit, and fewer understand it. In the end, my desire to encourage other motorcyclists to learn of this beautiful country and its people overcame my other concerns about writing such a book.

I hope to encourage those of you who are independent-minded to include Mexico in your future travel plans. This book has four itineraries, each with detailed routing notes which offer a wealth of varied experiences. You could easily mix and match options via connecting routes to plan a trip that suits your tastes, budget, and time requirements. I have also included a bit of history and other interesting tidbits to whet your appetite for exploring Mexico, even if it's not as an independent rider. My first experience motorcycling South of the Border was on a tour organized by Skip Mascorro of Pancho Villa Moto-Tours. It was a great introduction to the joys of riding in Mexico and I would recommend it highly— but whatever your method, go and enjoy.

As you will soon see, this guide does not rely on "direct routes." Instead, I have tried to seek out good motorcycle roads that are "off the beaten path." The hotels I recommend reflect the local culture rather than amenities. I have attempted to put you *into* Mexico instead of "in" Mexico.

This book was as accurate as I could make it at the time it was published. Things do change, however. Should you experience some change or discover something of interest that I have overlooked, or—God forbid—a mistake, please let me know at the publisher's address so we can update future editions.

I hope you have as much enjoyment reading and using this book as I have had writing it. After exploring Mexico, you can tell others of its wonders. *¡Vaya con Dios!*

Acknowledgments

Thanks to Dan and Judy Kennedy of Whitehorse Press for initially prodding and harassing me to take on this project. Their advice and support during the entire process was wonderful. To the editor, Lisa Dionne, for taking a very rough manuscript and, through talent and valiant effort, creating a document fit to be printed. To Skip Mascorro of Pancho Villa Moto-Tours for providing advice on routing and sharing his almost limitless knowledge of the area. To the guys with whom I have ridden in northern Mexico and shared many "secrets" over the years. And finally, thanks to Murray Cape who provided much insight and help in developing the Veracruz chapter. Thanks to you all!

There is some great riding in northern Mexico—but don't just take my word for it! (Photo by Lavoe Davis)

1 General Information

....

This book is a guide to good motorcycle roads and interesting places to visit in northern Mexico. I have also included some history, local attractions, and color to give a feel for where you are going. I did not intend for you to use this book alone, however. The first thing you will need is a good map. I find the American Automobile Association map of Mexico to be as good as any, and better than most. I also recommend you read and carry Joe Cummings' *Northern Mexico Handbook* to learn more history, culture, and local information. The Lonely Planet *Guidebook to Mexico* is another good resource. If you do some homework before you travel, your trip will be that much more enjoyable.

The routes I have chosen provide good riding and the chance to see a part of the country not normally traveled by *gringos*. I detail four itineraries which originate at the U.S. border. Each has very different features, and all can be covered in two weeks or less with a street motorcycle. The routes can be connected easily so you can mix and match your options to plan a trip that suits you. I have also described many interesting side trips and dual-sport opportunities.

At each overnight location I have selected a clean, adequate hotel that captures the local flavor and provides secure parking on site or nearby. Mexican towns are centered around a plaza in the heart of the city, which may be called a *zócalo, plaza de armas,* or *el jardín* depending on the town. Most hotels I recommend are on or near this main plaza. At most locations, many other hotels will be available. The American Automobile Association's *Mexico TravelBook* offers many other options that are suitable for American tastes. However, going to Mexico and staying in a chain hotel is not my bag. The Holiday Inn in Mazatlan is still a Holiday Inn. Instead, try the local hotels; you might miss some amenities, but staying in an 18th-century colonial home run by a local family could make your trip that much more memorable.

Safe, clean, and inexpensive accommodations will be available at all but the most remote locations. (Photo by Dan Kennedy)

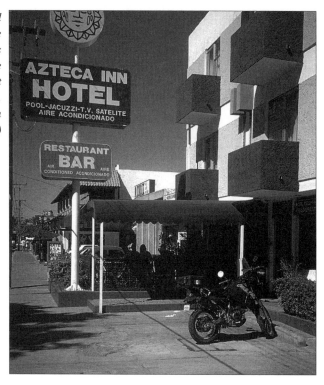

Although you certainly do not need to speak Spanish to travel in Mexico, any attempt on your part, no matter how feeble, will likely be met with friendly assistance. Taking a little time to familiarize yourself with some basic phrases will make your trip that much more enjoyable (see Appendices 1 and 2). In this book, we have chosen to render common Spanish words in italics, with the correct accent marks. Proper nouns and names have not been so distinguished.

Myths

Many people are reluctant to visit Mexico because of prevailing myths. For the most part, they are just that. None of these myths should prevent you from visiting Mexico. Here are a few:

Myth #1: Crime is rampant. The false assumption that one will encounter *banditos* around every curve keeps many people from visiting Mexico. Of course, crime does exist in

Mexico, but like anyplace else in the world, it tends to be more of a problem in larger cities and border towns. If you get robbed departing a bordello on a back street in Nuevo Laredo at 2 a.m., what did you expect? Leaving a helmet or other loose gear on your bike as you roam a city or village is not a good idea anywhere, but you are much less likely to experience a crime of violence in Mexico than you are in the U.S. I recommend you use common sense, remain aware of your surroundings, and take normal precautions. Unlike American hotels, most Mexican hotels provide secure overnight parking. And given a choice of a breakdown on a U.S. Interstate or Mexican back road (I've experienced both), I'd take Mexico any day. The people are generally friendly and eagerly offer assistance.

Myth #2: Harassment by officials is likely. Some differences in the culture and the legal system can present difficulties at times, but Mexican officials are making a real effort to crack down on drug activity and smuggling operations. Quite often you will come across roadblocks manned by the local or federal police, the army, or the Mexican equivalent of the D.E.A. These people are just trying to do their job. Since you

The grounds surrounding this remote Mexican hacienda make for a very pleasant evening stroll.

will be legal, have the necessary papers, and possess no contraband, you can just appreciate their efforts to ensure your safety, and smile. I have never been harassed by Mexican officials at these checkpoints.

Myth #3: Mexicans are lazy and unfriendly.   The economic situation in Mexico leaves many without a job, so you will see people standing around a lot. This does not equate to laziness, only nothing to do. It is the reason so many Mexicans take great risks to get into the U.S. and do work many of our citizens don't want. Treat the Mexicans you will meet with respect, as they are deserving of it.

The people of Mexico are some of the most friendly and helpful I have ever encountered. On occasion, I have experienced a distant attitude from locals, but this is unusual and may stem more from shyness, or maybe a prior bad experience with *gringos.* Take the time to learn a little of the language, and smile. Remember that the attitude you give is usually the one you will receive.

A gringo motorcyclist off the beaten path often becomes the object of a friendly and interested inspection by the locals. (Courtesy of Pancho Villa Moto-Tours)

Lunch can be a great adventure with tremendous rewards. Try something new! (Photo by Lavoe Davis)

Myth #4: You will get sick from contaminated water.

Many tourists suffer from mild digestive discomfort associated with drinking water whose regular bacteria is unfamiliar to their systems (tourists to the U.S. experience the same thing). I usually eat at roadside stands and local establishments without ill effect. However, your own personal tolerance to strange foods may vary. Use your own past experience as your guide.

A few general guidelines will prevent you from getting a bad case of the dreaded *turistas.* Drink only bottled water,

Northern Mexico has many high-speed toll roads, should you need to get somewhere in a hurry. (Photo by Dan Kennedy)

soft drinks, or other bottled liquids. Don't use ice unless it is made from purified water, and don't eat salads unless the dining facility uses purified water for washing food. Eat fruit you have to peel for yourself. Anything cooked is probably O.K.

It is my understanding that the proper treatment for this malady is to do nothing for the first 24 hours and try to let your body adjust. If the symptoms persist or get really bad, try over-the-counter drugs such as Pepto-Bismol or Imodium for the next 24 hours. After that, you'll need to use a prescription medication such as Lomotil; as a precaution, you might get your personal physician to provide you with a prescription before you leave home.

In spite of any precautions, I truly hope that you will make an attempt to enjoy Mexican food. What a wonderful sensation it is to have something placed in front of you that bears no relationship at all to what you think you ordered!

Crossing the Border

Usually, when entering Mexico with your documents in order, you can expect only a small bureaucratic delay. If you do not have the required documents, you simply will not be allowed to enter. Remember that you will be bringing two separate things into Mexico, yourself and your bike, and this will require two separate transactions.

Personal Documents. You must have a document verifying your citizenship and that of any passenger. A passport is best, but an original, certified copy of your birth certificate will do; a driver's license or voter's registration card will not, however. When you present your document to immigration, you will be issued a stamped *tarjeta de turista* (tourist card) which can be valid for up to 180 days with multiple entries. It is supposed to be returned as you depart Mexico, although I know no one who has ever done so. Please note that if you have a minor with you, you must have written permission from the other parent before they will be admitted to the country.

Motorcycle Paperwork. What you will be doing is getting a temporary permit to use your bike in Mexico without paying a duty, as well as a document promising to return this permit when you depart Mexico. You will need a title and registration in the same name that is on your driver's license, passport, and the credit card you will use to pay the entry fee ($11). Differences in the names that appear on these docu-

Be prepared for some bureaucratic delays at all border crossings. A smile and some enthusiasm for the trip ahead will help get you through the process.
(Photo by Judy Kennedy)

ments (e.g. full name vs. initials) can cause great difficulty and could prevent you from entering your bike. If the bike is not titled in your name or it has a lien on it, you will need a notarized letter from the other party permitting you to use the bike in Mexico.

Entry Procedures. After completing the necessary paperwork, you must make copies of your driver's license, credit card, passport, tourist card, and bike entry documents, including title, before going to the *banjercito* (bank) to have the documents reviewed and the charge made to your card. This sounds much more complicated than it actually is. These officials process millions of *gringos* each year and they will point you in the right direction. The important thing is to have your documents in order upon arrival.

After you pay the fee, someone will usually come out to confirm your VIN and license number, and then he will place a decal on your vehicle. At other entry points you will be given a decal and asked to confirm the VIN before applying it yourself. Be sure that all paperwork is correct; if there is an error, now is the time to correct it. You will then be ready to

One of the many reasons people return to Mexico again and again. (Courtesy of Mexico's Ministry of Tourism)

go, but keep all your documents handy as there will be a checkpoint a few miles down the road to verify everything. After this checkpoint, I usually put the documents in a safe place, although you may be asked for them at any time.

Exit Procedures. The laws state that upon exiting the country you must surrender all paperwork and the decal to the proper authorities, lest you be subject to fines up to the value of the duty on the vehicle (charged to the copy of the credit card you so kindly left behind). In the early years I never did this, usually because I was in a hurry and could find no one who knew what I was talking about. Now I do. The officials are making great strides in getting their database computerized and, in some locations, they now have the ability to trace all these transactions. Upon your return, I recommend you make a true effort to return these documents at the vehicle checkpoint a few miles from the border. If they will not take your documents there, they can direct you further. This is becoming increasingly important, especially if you intend to return to Mexico with the same vehicle. As an alternative, you might get a credit card issued with a very small credit limit so you will have some protection.

Insurance

The most important thing to remember is that your current American insurance policy will be invalid in Mexico. The second most important thing to remember is that Mexican law differs substantially from American law, in that you are presumed guilty until proven innocent. The smallest accident involving property damage, injury, or death can well result in a free, extended vacation, compliments of the Mexican government, until your case comes to trial. Not a good thought. You can eliminate all these problems by buying a Mexican insurance policy for the duration of your trip. I have had excellent experience with Sanborn's (tel. 210-686-0711 or 800-222-0158). They can write a policy on a daily basis. However, if you have planned multiple trips into Mexico, or are going to stay more than 30 days, inquire about a six-month policy, which is often cheaper. The standard policy offers liability and theft of vehicle (but not accessories). To my knowl-

This brand-new road into the Copper Canyon town of Divisadero is beautifully designed and built. (Photo by Lavoe Davis)

edge, collision and comprehensive are not available, although some policies issued directly from Mexico may include such coverage.

I also recommend an insurance policy that will provide for emergency medical evacuation. I use MEDJET (tel. 800-963-3538). The policy is good worldwide and costs approximately $150 per year to cover your entire family. Your travel agent can usually recommend other alternatives.

Driving in Mexico

The amount of time I have spent in Mexico and my experiences during those trips have made me comfortable riding there. We all have heard horror stories of cows and people in the road, of roads disappearing entirely as you top a hill or round a curve, and of Mexican drivers behaving erratically. Though they may contain a grain of truth, most of the stories, in my opinion, are greatly overstated.

Safe riding in any heavily-populated, unfamiliar area requires your being aware of changing road conditions, animals and people sharing the road, and other drivers whose behavior is typical for that area. The most important thing you can do is to take a good attitude. All too often, a *gringo* driver in Mexico acts as if all rules are off, taking chances and driving in a manner that he would never try in the U.S. I would suggest that you drive more conservatively while in Mexico than you might at home.

Rule number one should be *never, never, ride at night!* Even the highly regarded and capable Green Angels do not patrol the roads after dark. They know the conditions and dangers, and you'd do well to follow their example. Plan your day carefully and stop before sunset, even if you are not at your intended destination. I have broken this rule on occasion, but I've always felt the next day that the risk/reward ratio was not worth it.

Road Hazards. The condition of paved highways in northern Mexico has improved dramatically in recent years (especially the toll roads). Beware, however, that a long stretch of smooth blacktop is no guarantee that it will continue. As you round the next turn or go over the next hill you could find a pothole the size of a small moon crater—or the pavement might just end for a hundred yards or so. Also, it is not unusual to find a spot of diesel fuel along a curve in the road.

Vados can be fun! (Photo by Lavoe Davis)

Be careful—these guys are not always tethered.

Sometimes the shoulder of the road will be marked with pink spray paint as you approach. Skip Mascorro of Pancho Villa Moto-Tours theorizes that there must be more than two million trucks on Mexican highways, but they have only one million fuel caps for their tanks. Whatever the reason, be prepared.

Vados (dips) and *topes* (speed breaks) are other hazards. *Vados* exist to facilitate the movement of water during heavy rains. Subsequently, when dry, they are often full of sand, gravel, or other stuff you wouldn't want to hit at speed on a motorcycle. You will find *topes* upon entering or leaving a town or village, to make sure you slow down. Most larger towns and cities also have them placed strategically throughout the town. You can best handle these hazards by simply slowing down, paying attention to the signs, and never driving so fast that you cannot brake to a full stop within your range of vision. I have seen riders approach a clearly-marked *tope* at highway speed only to end up airborne—and yes, I have come close once or twice myself. Believe me, do this only once and *topes* will get your attention!

Mexico is free-range country, and you'll notice that large trucks will be equipped with what I call "cow crunchers." However, problems with livestock are much more common at night, and you should be traveling during daylight hours. Also, when traveling through crowded towns on market or *fiesta* days, realize that your motorcycle will not always be seen or heard. That guy looking at the pretty *señorita* could step out in front of you overcome with his ardor. You can minimize these problems by staying aware of the situation around you and adjusting your speed and alertness accordingly.

In Mexico, repairs to broken-down vehicles often occur on the roadway instead of at a repair shop. If you needed a new transmission, you'd order it and leave your truck on the road until it comes in. In the meantime, you might mark the

Throughout Mexico, roadside shrines mark spots where "souls have left this earth." Ride carefully, so there won't be a shrine with your name on it!

danger with a few stones (the good ones will be painted white), a small flag in a Coke bottle, or a limb from a nearby bush—*¡No problema!* Also, the vehicles on the road are generally older and in poorer repair than those in the States and stuff keeps falling off (bumpers, etc.). It has been my experience that this occurs most frequently as a vehicle rounds a curve or enters a tunnel. Early in your travels through Mexico you will also note the uncanny ability of the locals to get ten tons of cargo into a one and one-half ton pickup truck. Unfortunately, they usually arrive at their final destination with only nine tons of cargo remaining. The rest will be left on the roadway for your enjoyment. Stay alert!

Other Drivers. Mexico is the land of *machismo* and another driver on the road will not be likely to pass up any opportunity to prove his manhood. My wife has difficulty passing other motorists when they see she is a woman, as they will all but kill themselves and her to demonstrate that they possess superior driving abilities and a greater willingness to take risks. No passing zones seem to have no effect on their willingness to pass.

Remember also, you are the stranger and a close call could be due to your ignorance of local driving etiquette. One interesting (and potentially dangerous) custom is for the vehicle in front of you to turn on a left turn blinker to indicate to you that the road ahead is clear to pass. It has always eluded me how you determine whether this is a signal to pass, an indication of an upcoming left turn, or the fact that he just forgot to turn his blinker off. I personally never pass a vehicle without clear indication from my own senses that it is safe. Often, I will be with another rider who will give me the "high sign" to come on up, but no matter how much trust I have in his judgement, I wait until I can be sure on my own.

Adjusting Your Attitude. Attitude is the most important element in your having a safe trip on the roads and byways of Mexico. Some riders behave as if there are no rules, and they drive fast and take as many chances as they like. This is a recipe for disaster. While it is true that Mexican officials generally take a very lax attitude toward traffic rule enforcement, and the chances of a violation appearing on your home state

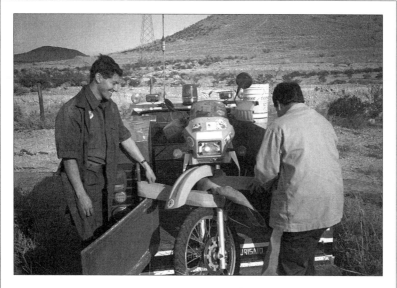

Green Angels

The Secretaria de Turismo operates a fleet of more than 1,000 trucks that patrol the major highways of Mexico to assist motorists with mechanical problems. These plainly-marked, green-and-white trucks usually have a two-man crew that is somewhat bilingual. They carry gasoline, oil, and other minor parts for on-road repairs, as well as a first-aid kit. They will be familiar with your route, know where the next service is, and have radio contact to get you the assistance you need. Although there is no charge for their services, you should offer a tip. If you are on the side of the road and can find a phone, call 91-800-90-392 to have the nearest crew sent to your aid.

I once threw a chain 70 miles from the nearest town. As I was standing on the side of the road with the sun setting, wondering what to do, and reluctant to leave my bike, the green-and-white truck pulled up. After we reviewed the options, they loaded the bike into the back of the truck and we proceeded to the nearest hotel. Since they were not satisfied with the parking security at the hotel, one angel who lived nearby insisted that he take my motorcycle to his house for safekeeping. The next morning, which was his day off, he came to the hotel and we went to an open-air market where he located a chain that would work. We then returned to his house where he installed the chain. He refused a tip. *¡Angeles Verdes!*

driving record or insurance company records is almost non-existent, when you are flat on your back on the pavement or in a ditch hurting and wondering how you are going to get home without that beautiful bike, these considerations mean little. Plan your days to allow plenty of time for roadside stops to see the sights and visit in small towns. Leave the cowboy stuff to the locals. You are much more likely to arrive back home safe and sound without unnecessary wear and tear on your nerves (or relationships) by making this attitude adjustment.

In spite of all the warnings I have given in this section, I have been told that the average insurance claim rate for foreigners driving in Mexico is about two percent—much lower than in the U.S. Of course, these facts may be somewhat misleading, as accidents are often handled on the spot with a quick exchange of pesos and no police involvement. But whatever the case, if you slow down, avoid unnecessary chances, adjust your attitude, and be alert to possible hazards, you should have a safe and enjoyable time riding in Mexico.

You can't always judge the resourcefulness of a mechanic by the
appearance of his garage

Mexican Weather Statistics—Yearly Averages			
City	Rainfall (inches)	High Temp. (F)	Low Temp. (F)
Ciudad Juarez	11	107	33
Cordoba	90	93	57
Chihuahua	16	102	34
Dolores Hidalgo	12	114	32
Durango	16	95	35
Fortin de las Flores	88	102	32
Guanajuato	30	97	36
Guaymas	11	112	46
Hermosillo	10	112	32
Jalapa	62	96	40
La Paz	29	107	50
Mazatlan	33	94	54
Mexico City	24	90	34
Nogales	16	102	28
Puebla	33	88	30
Saltillo	14	102	48
San Miguel de Allende	21	100	34
Veracruz	64	100	51

When to Go

What will the weather be like? Good question. Seasonal temperatures in Mexico will vary greatly depending on your altitude and distance from water. As a general rule, the higher, the cooler, and winter weather is generally cooler as well. Although the winter warmth of Mazatlan and Veracruz is most welcome to American tourists, these tropical places become hot and steamy in midsummer. The higher elevations of San Miguel de Allende and the other colonial cities offer refreshing nighttime temperatures, but most hotels and eating establishments will not have air conditioning for the occasional heat wave. The desert could have scorching hot days with cool nights or you could encounter a cold front from Canada that will chill your bones all the way to the Tropic of Cancer. From a temperature standpoint, it is generally better to plan your trips in the spring and fall to avoid any extremes.

Rainfall varies again with the altitude. However, you are more likely to encounter rain between midsummer and early fall. This may amount to a few inches over a period in the desert highlands to daily afternoon "monsoons" on the coasts. Always carry raingear whatever the time of year or destination, and I recommend a light jacket for all but midsummer, low-elevation trips. Plan for very cool temperatures at high altitude destinations and carry some shorts, a bathing suit, and tee shirts anytime you plan to visit the coastal areas.

When is the best time to visit Mexico? Whenever you can find the time.

Gasoline

The only service station you will find in Mexico is PEMEX. This is the government-controlled national oil company. As anywhere in the world, when the government gets involved, service usually deteriorates. While great improvements have been made in the past few years, gas stations can still be few and far between and they may have no supplies when you pull in. I recommend always running on the top half of your tank. When filling up, you may encounter an all-too-common scam I call "the 100-peso trick." If you owe less than 100 pesos and you give the attendant a 200-peso note, make sure he does not give you change for only a 100-peso note. When you gently remind him that you gave him a 200-peso note, he will "remember" immediately and give you the remaining change.

Money

The Mexican unit of currency is the peso. It fluctuates on a daily basis and has currently been running about ten pesos to the U.S. dollar. You can get pesos at almost all border crossings, but if you run short while in Mexico, banks usually offer the best exchange rates, although their exchange service may only be available during the morning hours even when the bank is open in the afternoon. ATMs are available in major cities and they typically offer a great rate of exchange.

Credit cards are useful at many locations, but don't count on hotels accepting them. PEMEX stations do not accept credit cards, so plan on using cash for your gasoline purchases. In more remote areas, *cambio* (change) is not always available. Try and keep several small-denomination peso coins available for these instances.

Navigation

Road signs in northern Mexico are usually very good. Instead of using a highway number, Mexican road signs are usually labeled with a destination, much as they are in Europe. When entering larger Mexican cities, however, it can get very hectic. Signs will be in Spanish, people will be everywhere, and roads will double back on themselves without any semblance of a grid pattern. In these instances, I often use the "taxi trick" to lower my blood pressure. Just write the name and address of your hotel or the name of the central plaza on a piece of paper and put it in a handy place. When you are lost and have had enough, stop and show it to a taxi driver and ask to be led to your hotel. Make sure you determine the price beforehand—usually a buck or two. Obviously, you can use this

In northern Mexico, modern gas stations exist right alongside beautiful old stone churches.

same method to get out of a city and onto the main highway to your next destination.

Hotels

Mexican hotels differ from what you will find in the U.S. Unless they are in the "budget" category, you can expect them to be clean and have all the basic amenities. If you intend to stay in a lower-end hotel, be sure and ask if they have *agua caliente* (hot water), and have a look at the room before checking in. One thing you will notice at once is the lack of a washcloth in the bath. If this is important to you, bring one from home. Some of the hotels recommended in this book are very old and located on a busy central square; ear plugs can sometimes come in handy.

Medical Tips

Medical care and drugs are readily available in Mexico. In fact, many medicines that are only available by prescription in the U.S. can be obtained over the counter at a Mexican pharmacy (notice the ads for Viagra). Nevertheless, by bringing any prescription drugs you use regularly (in their original

A good night's sleep will be easier if your bike is inside a closed courtyard just outside your door.

containers) you can save yourself much time and effort. Other common remedies readily found at home may not be available in Mexico (Rolaids, for example). Plan on taking along a supply of anything you use routinely, as well as a few "emergency" items.

Motorcycle Repair

I am continually amazed at the ingenuity and competence of Mexican "shade-tree" mechanics. Electrical and electronic problems can be difficult, but if you have a simple mechanical problem, they will figure out a way to get you back on the road. Generally in Mexico, few dealerships have repair facilities, so an independent repair shop will usually be your best bet. Most major cities will have a parts supply store that stocks an amazing number of parts for almost every common model of bike. When the mechanic determines the problem, he will send a runner to purchase the part. *¡No problema!*

Take along a few spare parts if you know beforehand that your model bike is prone to certain problems. If space allows, a spare chain or master link can often be a real ace in the hole.

Choosing Your Bike

This is like the question of which bike is the "best." I usually travel in Mexico on a Kawasaki KLR 650 because it is reliable and simple to repair, and it gives me dual-sport capability. However, I have also traveled in Mexico on a Honda VFR and a BMW R1100RS. Do remember, however, the more complicated the machine, the more difficulty you're likely to encounter in obtaining repairs. In my opinion, all routes described in this book can be ridden on a heavy dresser. I point out a small number of dirt side trips for those who wish.

Evidence of the labor of Indian slaves can be found everywhere in northern Mexico.

2 A Brief History

The following is a very brief outline of Mexican history. It is not intended to be complete, only to give you a feel for the background of the people you will encounter during your ride. Please utilize other sources to fully appreciate the long, wonderful, and often tragic story of Mexico and it's people.

It appears that Mexico was originally settled more than 15,000 years ago by people migrating from Asia across the land bridge at the Bering Strait. For many thousands of years, these **hunters and wanderers** left little sign of their existence. Starting about 3500 B.C.E., however, villages and farms started to appear, and it was these people who formed the bedrock of Mexico's Indian population.

Between 1200 and 500 B.C.E., the **Olmecs** flourished on the Gulf coast and left us with many signs of an advanced civilization, as well as many mysteries that are the subject of much debate among scholars today. The Olmecs were noted for carving massive stone faces with Oriental features. Where did the features on these carvings originate? We do know that the art, religion, and beliefs of the Olmecs had a significant impact on later, better-known cultures. Their civilization perished for unknown reasons, perhaps as the result of war. Today it is believed that the Mayas of the south were direct descendants of the Olmecs.

Another great civilization of northern Mexico was centered in **Teotiuacan,** near modern day Mexico City, and it existed until the 7th century. In 400 C.E., the population of this city was estimated at more than 200,000. These people had a written language and a complicated mathematical system. Again, the reason for the downfall of this civilization is unknown. Perhaps it overgrew its capacity to feed itself or was conquered by aggressors. This site came to have important religious significance to the later Aztecs, who called it the **"Birthplace of the Gods."**

The Aztec era in Mexico began in the first half of the 14th century. These wandering people, led by priests, had been looking for a sign, **an eagle perched on a cactus with a snake in its mouth,** and they found it near the present-day site of Mexico City. This symbol is on the Mexican flag even today. By the mid-15th century, the **Aztec** had become the dominant player in the region, forming an alliance with two other powerful tribes to rapidly conquer outlying tribes and districts. Although theirs was a very advanced civilization, the Aztecs believed that **human sacrifice to the gods** was the only way to gather favors and ensure their continued existence. Their ready domination of others and bloodthirst for tributes ultimately made it easy for the Spanish to find allies against this awesome nation.

The early Aztecs wandered in search of an eagle perched on a cactus eating a snake. This symbol appears on the Mexican flag today. (Courtesy of Pancho Villa Moto-Tours)

In 1519, a 34-year old Spaniard named **Hernan Cortes** led an unauthorized expedition of approximately 550 men in search of the rumored wealth of Mexico. At this time, the Aztec controlled an area stretching from the Yucatan Peninsula to the Pacific, with at least 350 individual nations as their subjects. The Spanish landed near present-day Veracruz, but when the men learned of the power of the Aztec many wanted to depart—a problem Cortes overcame by **having all the boats burned.**

The Spanish had an unforseen advantage, however, in the Aztec legend of the god **Quetzalcoatl,** a wise, kind, fair-skinned, bearded ruler who had sailed east in a boat because of an indiscretion which had disgraced him. Coincidentally, the Aztec believed he would return specifically in the year 1519 to retake his rightful throne. Since **Cortes fit the picture quite well,** the Aztec delayed any actions against the Spanish until they were sure that Cortes was not, indeed, Quetzalcoatl. The Spanish also unwittingly introduced smallpox, malaria, and other **European diseases,** such as STDs, to the non-resistant native population, with devastating results. By the time the *conquistadors* defeated the Aztec under their last ruler, **Cuauhtemoc,** the population had been decimated by these diseases. So it came to be that the very small Spanish forces were able to overcome such a powerful nation. Thus began more than 300 years of colonial rule in Mexico.

From their central Mexico base, the **Spanish** continued their explorations and conquests. The Spanish domination of Mexico was driven by both **greed and religious zeal.** The land was divided into large *encomiedas,* rights to land and slaves. Many of the padres tried to stop the horrible abuses to which the enslaved natives were subjected, but they were not successful. The discovery of the huge **La Bufa silver mine** at Zacatecas in 1540 further fueled Spanish conquest and the era of exploitation rapidly grew. Exploration and claims for land eventually reached as far north as **Colorado.** Native Indians were forced to mine the newly found riches and the church gained great power and wealth along with the governing families. The padres who accompanied the *conquistadors* **established missions** along these routes to convert the "pagan" Indians. By 1605 the Indian population had been reduced from an estimated 25 million at the time of the Spanish landing, to just over one million by disease, murder, and mistreatment.

In this new order, a person's **place in society** was determined by skin color, birthplace, and parentage. At the top were people who were **Spanish-born,** known as *peninsulares.* These people obviously represented a very small percentage of the population, but they controlled the country and its wealth. They were considered nobility in Nueva España. Next were the *criollos,* **born of Spanish parents in Mexico**. This was the class that developed the mining, ran businesses, and very quickly demanded political power. At the bottom of the ladder were the *mestizos* (people of mixed race) and, of course, the **native Indians.** Although the development of northern Mexico continued at an almost frantic pace for nearly 300 years, unrest and resentment were growing.

On September 16, 1810, **Father Miguel Hidalgo,** a parish priest in Dolores, made his now-famous **Grito de Dolores.** In this call for independence, Hidalgo urged the people to "recover the lands stolen 300 years ago from your forefathers by the hated Spaniards." The town would later be renamed **Dolores Hidalgo** in honor of him, the "Father of the Revolution." The guiding principles of the revolution included the abolition of royal privileges and ownership, the abolition of slavery, and sovereignty for the people. For the next 12 years fighting would continue and many of today's Mexican heroes would emerge, among them **Ignacio Allende** and **Vicente Guerrero.** The revolution was successful in 1821, and in 1824 a constitution was enacted. Mexico's first president, **Guadalupe Victoria,** was sworn into office.

A stable government proved hard to obtain, however. Between 1833 and 1855, the presidency of Mexico changed hands 33 times and the story is rife with assassinations, intrigue, and infighting by the various political and military factions. Eleven of these presidential terms were held by **Antonio Lopez de Santa Anna.** After Mexico had won its independence from the Spanish, the Mexican government had encouraged U.S. citizens to abandon their citizenship and

*The Catholic
Church had a
great influence on
Mexico's colonial
history.*

settle in Mexico's northern territories, to become citizens of
the new republic of Mexico. Although it was supposed to
help "civilize" these northern areas, these Anglo-American
settlers viewed Mexicans as second-class citizens in their
own country and hence treated them very poorly. Soon they
wanted an **independent nation** of their own. When the
"Texicans" declared independence in 1836, Santa Anna and
his army moved north to reclaim their lands. After defeating
the insurgents at the **Alamo,** Santa Anna was surprised and
defeated at San Jacinto.

This statue of Pancho Villa in Zacatecas is only one of many you will find throughout Mexico. (Courtesy of Pancho Villa Moto-Tours)

After his defeat, Santa Anna signed a treaty recognizing the **new nation of Texas.** However, the terms of the treaty were almost immediately questioned by both sides. Unfortunately, neither side could produce a copy of the treaty to back up their claims. The most important dispute was over the location of the actual **border between Texas and Mexico.** The Texans claimed all the land north of the Rio Grande River. The Mexicans claimed the border was further north, at the Nuches River. After Texas was accepted into the United States in 1845, U.S. troops headed south to rightfully claim "their" territory, setting off the **Mexican-American War.** The war ended when **General Winfield Scott** landed at Veracruz and marched on to capture Mexico City. The young military cadets who defended Chapultepec Castle, the last place of resistance in Mexico City, are known as **Los Niños Heroes** and they are remembered every September 13th in a ceremony at their monument in Chapultepec Park. As a result of the war and an additional purchase of land from the Mexicans, the United States gained the territory that now makes up Texas, California, Utah, Colorado, New Mexico, and Arizona, and **Mexico lost over 50 percent of its land.** As a result of all this, Santa Anna was finally thrown out of office for the last time.

In 1861, a Zapotec Indian named **Benito Juarez** was elected president. From an orphaned home and abject poverty, he had worked hard and become a lawyer. The story of his accession to this high office against almost overwhelming odds make him one of **Mexico's most beloved historical figures.** You will find many streets and plazas throughout Mexico bearing his name. Juarez had an ambitious agenda of education reform and established the *rurales,* a rural police force. Although he made many economic reforms, Juarez faced enormous problems with **foreign debt** and declared a two-year moratorium on their repayment. Millions were owed to France, and **French Emperor Napoleon III** seized the opportunity to add to his empire, invading Veracruz in late 1861.

An early Mexican victory over the French forces at the city of Puebla on May 5, 1862 is now celebrated each year as the **Cinco de Mayo.** Although they never succeeded in com-

pletely conquering Mexico, the French were eventually able
to take over the central sections of the country, including
Mexico City, and Napoleon sent the Austrian archduke,
Maximilian of Hapsburg to be the emperor of Mexico.
Shortly thereafter, however, France began withdrawing
troops in response to pressure from the U.S. With the vast
majority of his forces returned to Europe, the emperor had no
support. The Mexican Army prevailed and defeated the
French at **Queretaro** during May of 1867. Maximilian was
shot by a firing squad and Juarez was restored to office.

For almost a third of a century, 1876–1910, Mexico was in
the hands of a dictator, **Porfirio Diaz.** He quickly developed
the country with industry, a railway system, and foreign in-
vestment, and the gap between the "have's" and "have-nots"
rapidly widened. Large **land holdings** were established
where the common man was basically a slave to the owner.
One such holding exceeded seven million acres! As conditions continued to deteriorate for the average Mexican, the
country once again became ripe for revolution.

Most Mexican cities will greet you with imposing monuments to their
culture and history.

1910 would bring on **six years of intense fighting** for control of Mexico. Unless you are a scholar of Mexican history, it is truly hard to follow the various and often changing alliances during this period. The names of famous leaders and generals are revered throughout Mexico today. **Francisco Madero, Emiliano Zapata,** and **Pancho Villa** were leaders of various factions during this time. Finally, in 1917 a stable government was established and the constitution that was enacted is still in force today.

Private ownership of land in Mexico became a right, not a privilege, and land seized during the Porfirio years was restored to local communities so the people could work it. Foreign ownership of land was limited. A minimum wage was established and workers were allowed to form unions. The power of the church was reduced. The reform continued through the presidency of **Lazaro Cardenas** in the 1930s with the nationalization of the foreign-owned oil companies giving birth to PEMEX, the government-owned oil company that exists today.

In 1929 the **Institutional Revolutionary Party (PRI)** was formed and it has maintained control of the Mexican government to this day. Tales of corruption in the election process abound, however. Whatever the case, Mexico has now enjoyed more than seventy years of peace, although economic ups and downs have caused problems with the economy, and scandals and stories of corruption have often caused setbacks. In spite of these misfortunes, northern Mexico now has a good infrastructure and many industrial facilities, and the government has made great efforts to preserve its heritage. In recent years, the popularity of the opposition parties has grown and their candidates have filled several major positions in the government. Some predict we may see a change in Mexico's controlling party soon.

You can eat your lunch on the plaza beside a mission church that offers a glimpse into the past.

3 Customs and Habits

●●●

You travel to a strange country to see the sights, meet new people, and learn their ways. In Mexico, many things are different than they are at home. Please take the time to read Carl Franz's *The People's Guide to Mexico* (John Muir Publications) before you go. It will greatly add to the enjoyment of your trip.

Eating

This can be one of the great joys of traveling in northern Mexico. Don't expect to see what is available at "Mexican" restaurants in the U.S.; that is Tex-Mex, not true Mexican food. Most larger Mexican cities now have American chain restaurants. You will see the familiar Golden Arches, as well as Domino's pizza delivery motorcycles twisting through traffic. You will also find other types of "foreign" food in the larger cities (Italian, Chinese, etc.). I suggest you do not eat in any of these places unless you are homesick. You came here to see Mexico, you should taste it too.

Mexican eating opportunities run the full gamut, from the most elegant establishments to the most humble street vendors. Try and eat with the locals. A small cafe off the plaza will provide you with a great quantity of food at a reasonable price. Eating a freshly caught fish in a thatched roofed, four-table place looking out on the ocean can be a real pleasure. The folks at the *gringo* hotel a few miles down the road will be eating the same thing with none of the ambiance at four times the price.

Meal times in Mexico are a little later than those in the U.S. If you want to get on the road at 7:00 a.m., better get some sweets or fruit the night before as few places open before this hour. Lunch is generally taken between 1:00 and 3:00 p.m. and dinner starts after 9:00 p.m. If you choose to eat earlier, you will probably be eating alone or with other *gringos*. To a Mexican, a meal is more than just the food, it is an occasion that can take several hours to enjoy. Service will be slow as the food is generally prepared only after it has been ordered, and *la cuenta* (the check) will not be presented until you ask for it. (If your Spanish is poor, pretend to sign your palm; a few minutes later the check will appear.)

Since food selection and preparation reflect regional preferences, few general statements can be made regarding what you will find available. Obviously, when you are near the coast you can expect the seafood to be wonderful and fresh. *Pescado frito* is a whole fish fried well done. *Filete de pescado* (filet of fish) is also generally fried. An all-time favorite, *huachinago a la veracruzana,* is a grilled filet of red snapper covered with a red sauce and olives. Lobster tacos are often offered by street vendors near the sea, but these are best enjoyed earlier in the day when they are fresh.

A staple of the Mexican diet is *frijoles* (refried beans), and they will be included with just about every meal, including

The television is a constant feature in small Mexican eateries and you can expect the volume to be full on!

breakfast. Unless you request *pan* (bread) when ordering your meal, expect to be served *tortillas,* thin, round, cooked cakes of corn or wheat flour. These little cakes are survival food for the poorest Mexicans, and with a little butter and salt they often make up an entire meal. It is unusual to find grain-fed beef offered in all but the very best eating establishments. As a result, beef will be tougher than what you are accustomed to. It is usually sliced very thin and cooked well done. Try the *bistec milanesa* which is similar to a "chicken-fried" steak in the U.S. To find out more about what else you might encounter, see Appendix 2: On the Menu.

While in Mexico, order what you think you want and then wait for the surprise!

Drinking

Booze is readily available throughout northern Mexico. Domestic beers, wines, brandy, and the infamous tequila can be

You can get delicious, inexpensive food from street vendors. (Photo by Lavoe Davis)

Tequila

The native drink of Mexico, tequila, dates back at least to the Aztecs and maybe even earlier. Tequila is made from the hearts of the *agave tequilana weber* (blue agave) plant, and only plants grown in certain areas (primarily Jalisco) are allowed to be utilized in the production of any product called "tequila." A blue agave takes ten or more years to mature. After harvesting the plant, the heart is removed, baked in an earth-covered oven, chopped into small pieces, and ground to extract its juice. This juice is then fermented in ceramic pots and distilled to produce a "no frills" product. Much of the tequila production in Mexico today continues to be done by hand in small distilleries that use the same methods they did hundreds of years ago.

Most tequilas are 51 percent distilled, fermented juice of the blue agave and the rest is either sugar cane juice or other agave extracts. Top quality brands are 100 percent blue agave and will be so noted on the label. All tequilas are approximately 40 percent alcohol; it is the flavor and smoothness that sets them apart. There are four types of tequila: basic "white" (or silver) tequila is the straight, unaged stuff without any additions; "gold" tequila is still unaged, but contains a color-enhancing additive (usually caramel); tequila *reposado* (rested), which has been aged for a short period of time and coloring and flavorings are usually added; and tequila *añejo* (aged) which has been kept in oak barrels for at least a year after distillation, and color and flavoring are usually added. While tequila drinkers outside Mexico are probably familiar with only the major brands (Jose Cuervo and Sauza, to name two), there are many local brands (comparable to estate-bottled wines) that claim to be much superior to the mass-produced variety available outside Mexico.

The traditional way of drinking tequila involves licking a small amount of salt (to raise a protective coating of saliva on the tongue) and taking a straight shot of the liquor, followed by sucking on a lime wedge (which cleanses the tongue of the tequila residues). A *norteamericano* invention, the margarita, made of tequila, lime juice, and Cointreau served in a salt-rimmed glass is considered a "sissy" way of consuming tequila by most Mexicans, as it dilutes the flavor of the liquor. A frozen margarita is considered almost a sin. Whatever way you decide to try this national drink, be careful—it has been the downfall of many a *gringo* or *gringa* who has tried to keep up with the locals! ∎

found in any town and often at roadside stands. Mexican drinking habits generally reflect the social status of the participants. At the top of society, men and women might have a glass of wine with their lunch at a high-class restaurant. At the bottom are the *cantinas* where women are not welcome and the rear wall often serves as the restroom. Unless you are adventurous, stay away from the *cantinas.*

Mexican feelings toward getting drunk also have two extremes. On one hand, to be *borracho* (drunk) is not acceptable; on the other, it is required. You will see little drunkeness on a day-to-day basis, but during a *fiesta* or wedding reception expect it to be the norm. In fact, by not getting drunk at a wedding you may doom the marriage! Also, many Indian rituals require the participants get drunk. Use your judgement, as you would at home, as to where and how much to drink.

Machismo

Machismo (manliness) is a trait that runs throughout Mexico. You will encounter it on the road when a bus driver passes you on a hill or blind curve just to prove he has more courage than you. It will come to the forefront at any slight or perceived slight to a man's virility. This might include your showing disbelief regarding a statement that is obviously a complete lie. The best way to avoid trouble is to just mind your own business and be friendly. Let the other guy be the better man.

For women, Mexican *machismo* creates other problems. The typical Mexican man sees his mother, wife, daughters, sisters, and other female relatives as pure, sweet, and to be ever-protected from danger and the real world. They are treated with the utmost courtesy and respect. All other women are basically fair game for this man among men. This is usually reflected by his making a lewd suggestion upon encountering a single woman, although this will be more a show for his friends than an actual invitation. The best way to deal with this behavior is to avoid situations where it may occur. If possible, travel in the company of others, dress conservatively, and carry yourself with dignity. Should you encounter a display of *machismo,* ignore it and continue on your way.

Dress

Arriving in a small village or even medium-sized city in your riding gear will make you the focus of attention. Often you will be asked about the purpose of it all and your gear may be touched and examined closely. Enjoy the attention and be patient. What you wear when you are not in riding gear is more important, however. Mexicans are very intolerant of any nudity or improper showing of skin. Men are rarely without a

An encounter with a tour group will give you the opportunity to make new friends.

A siesta is possible in just about any environment. (Photo by Dwight Carlos Hughes)

shirt except when they are working in the fields or at the beach. Women generally dress from head to toe. A *gringo,* or more importantly, a *gringa* without proper coverage, as deemed by the locals, will invite lewd comments, dismay, and maybe even a warning from the local police to change your attire. Dress conservatively, except at the international resorts. As throughout the world, larger cities used to seeing stupid tourists dressed in outlandish costumes are more tolerant.

Realize that the display of the Mexican flag or even its colors on clothing is a no-no. I was once traveling with a friend who had a Mexican flag bandana tied around his neck as we were entering the country. The officials refused to process his paperwork until it was removed. Also, articles of clothing purchased from an Indian are best worn after leaving the area, as there may be meanings in the designs that you do not understand.

Siestas

Siesta is one of my most favorite Mexican customs. In Mexico, the main meal of the day is lunch, and this is followed by an afternoon nap—a wonderful custom that originated in Spain. It can cause some difficulty for the traveler, in that most of the shops and stores (including banks) will be closed from 1:00 p.m. to 4:00 p.m., reopening again later for several hours. When you are on the road, plan around this custom; when you are having a rest day, enjoy it. However, be warned that *siestas* can become addictive!

Beggars and Street Vendors

Mexico is a poor country, but you will be amazed at the ways these ingenious people have discovered to try and make a peso or two. At service stations, children will be trying to clean your windshield with a dirty rag, or sell you trinkets or candy. Also, in the larger cities it is common to see Indian women with babies sitting on the sidewalks begging, although I have been told that many of these Indian women are

Buy a sack of oranges and make some friends. Then give them away down the road and make more friends.

Can we get this on the bike?

trucked into the cities in the morning by a "manager" and most of their daily take goes to him. Let your conscience be your guide. A few pesos here and there will not inflate the cost of your trip that much and may do some good. Personally, I never give to a beggar, but if someone is offering a service or goods, I might make a small purchase, say of some candies or gum, and then give it to others as I travel down the road. If you do not want what is being offered, a friendly, *"No, gracias,"* with a smile will send them on their way.

Prostitution and the "No-Tell" Motel

Prostitution is a legal and accepted practice in most of Mexico. The health hazards of partaking in this activity are the same here as they are all over the world. A Mexican bordello, usually located on the outskirts of town, is considered a place to meet friends, have a few drinks, and pass a pleasant evening. I have been told that many bordellos make most of their profit from customers who just come in to drink and gossip

You can't have a fiesta without balloons.

with their friends. Should you wish to visit one of these places, just ask a taxi driver to take you.

Another common feature of most Mexican towns is the "no-tell" motel, usually located on the outskirts of town, surrounded by a high fence. The rooms have individual parking garages with curtains that can be drawn to hide the identity of the vehicle within. Although these are sometimes bordellos, most are commonly used for "meetings" between a Mexican man and his mistress. They can offer a suitable overnight stop for a traveler, as they are clean and quiet and parking is secure. When inquiring about a room, make it very clear that you want the room for the entire night and that is the only service you will need. Because of their purpose, these places usually do not have restaurant facilities.

Bargaining

As a general rule, prices for goods and services in Mexico are subject to negotiation, except in larger department stores and *mercados.* (Be assured that the price you will pay for a Coke on the side of the road will be higher than what the locals pay. However, it is generally not negotiable.) When making any purchase at a market or buying a souvenir, bargaining is an accepted and expected practice. Even at an upscale jewelry store in a tourist destination such as San Miguel de Allende, the price shown on the item won't be the selling price. On smaller purchases, haggling is probably not worth the effort, but on larger ones it can save you up to 50 percent of the original asking price. Enter into and enjoy the give and take of this process; understand up front that the seller will make a profit on any transaction, whatever your level of skill.

Fiestas

The opportunity for a party or celebration is never overlooked in Mexico. If there is no reason for a *fiesta,* one will be found. *Fiestas* are often distinguished with colorful clothing, children everywhere running and playing, music that reaches higher than normal pitches, and fireworks. In fact, your first indication of a *fiesta* may be your being awakened to the sound of fireworks! Many *fiestas* are associated with church holidays or particular saints' days. Important dates in Mexican history, such as Cinco de Mayo, or even a person's birthday might be celebrated with a *fiesta.* When you encounter a *fiesta,* stop and enjoy the activities. It will certainly add to the richness of your visit.

Bullfights

Whatever your personal feeling toward this activity, bullfighting is both a fact of life in Mexico and a much-loved pastime. Called either the *corrida de toros* (the running of the bulls) or *la fiesta brava* (the brave festival), bullfights take place on Sunday afternoons in most major cities.

Many rural villages have a bullring, some only used once or twice a year. The major rings attract more accomplished *matadors* and better bulls, for a much grander spectacle. In northern Mexico, the fights in Mazatlan and Zacatecas are considered the top of the line.

Bullfighting can trace its history back to 3000 B.C.E. on the island of Crete, and it began its refinement on the Iberian peninsula more than 4,000 years ago. The first "formal" bullfights are believed to have been performed for the entertainment of the Romans. The manner and order of modern bullfights can be traced back more than 500 years to Spain.

A bullfight is not a contest between man and bull, but rather a contest between the various *matadors* performing that day. Usually, three *matadors* compete against each other, each facing two bulls at different times. The killing of the bull is not the measure of the performance, but rather the bravery of the *matador,* as demonstrated by his not moving away from a charging bull, the skill with which he handles the cape and sword, and the compassion he shows by putting the bull away at the proper time in a quick and clean manner. The spirit of the bull contributes greatly to the quality of the performance. On occasion, when a bull has shown unusual ability, he is spared and retired to stud.

The bulls, *toros de Iidia,* are a special breed that are highly combative and quick to anger. They are not trained for the fight, but come by these traits naturally. If they are judged fit at the age of two, they are turned loose to run wild until about the age of four when they are ready for their day in the ring.

The flesh of the bull is sold after the kill or, quite often, given to the needy.

A bullfight follows a definite order, starting with a "call to arms," usually a Spanish *paso doble* with the *matador* and his assistants entering the ring in all their splendor to salute the crowds and the fight authorities. Then the bull is released into the ring and prepared for battle by assistants who tire and weaken him by placing long lances, called *picas,* into his shoulders. He is then further prepared by the placing of three pairs of darts into the shoulders. This is, perhaps, the most dangerous part of the entire process and quite technical.

During the final act, called the *suerte de muleta,* the *matador* and bull face each other one-on-one. This climax can last no longer than 16 minutes. If the bull is not finished by then, it is led from the ring and promptly killed by a butcher. The *matador* will start with a large cape and work the bull closer and closer to his body in a series of daring passes. At the

The Day of the Dead, on October 31st of each year, is a cause for celebration in Mexico, as families honor and respect their departed loved ones. Many people actually spend the night in the cemetery.

proper time, as judged by the *matador,* he will exchange his large cape for a small cape and a sword, and ask the authorities for permission to continue. Again and again the bull will charge this small cape until he is almost completely exhausted. On the final charge, the *matador* will go over the horns and, hopefully, deliver the fatal thrust.

For most Americans, the costumes, pomp, and spectacle of the event far overshadow the ending. Something like a Super Bowl accompanied by *¡Olés!*

Asking for Directions

Mexicans are eager to please—but this can often lead to trouble and misunderstandings. If you make a request that someone cannot possibly fulfill, you will not get a "no;" instead, you will get a well-intended wrong answer. This becomes particularly troubling when asking for directions. Even when a person has no idea of where you wish to go, he will give it his best shot. Because of this, it may be best to ask several people for directions and hope to get some confirmation by consensus. Also, this can be troubling when requesting a service of someone. Even when they know it cannot possibly be done today or tomorrow, they will tell you that it can be done rather than disappoint you. Be aware of this trait and factor it into all your dealings.

Time

The idea of being "on time" does not exist in most Mexican environments. Life is to be enjoyed, not rushed. *Mañana* literally means "tomorrow;" in reality, it means "sometime." If a restaurant is to open at 7:00 a.m., that generally means that the staff will show up about that time and begin preparations for serving customers sometime after that. The best way to handle this situation is be prepared for it and relax.

La Mordida

The *mordida* (a "little bite"—a bribe) is an old custom in Mexico. Traditionally, it has been the way a poorly-paid public servant made up for his low salary, as well as a means for a traveler (or resident) to avoid prolonged and time-consuming bureaucratic experiences.

When you ask for directions you'll always get an answer—and sometimes it will even be correct!

When I first started traveling to Mexico in 1969, it was standard procedure to "give" the inspector one U.S. dollar, after which he would clear your luggage by marking it with a piece of chalk without ever opening it. Today, this is no longer the case. The Mexican government has made great efforts to eliminate the *mordida* as a way of life and has been quite successful, particularly at border crossings, where you will find prominently-posted signs warning that it is a crime to offer an official any gratuity for rendering a service. It is my more recent experience that this is rigidly enforced. If you have your paperwork in order and have no contraband and nothing to hide, you might experience a bureaucratic delay, but money will not help to hurry it along. In fact, it can cause big problems. If you are ever uncertain about a situation, ask to see the *jefe* (boss).

Sometimes, at a checkpoint or inspection station, an official may ask you for a dollar or a cigarette in order to clear you through. Instead of offering a *mordida,* I usually pretend

A rare meeting with fellow bikers will give you an opportunity to share experiences and adventures.

not to understand, and I have always been successful in continuing on my way. Never paid, always passed—even when army personnel asked for a *mordida* so I could continue traveling through Chiapas in the midst of the uprising in early 1994.

However, I will admit, all rules have exceptions. A *mordida* is still sometimes the quickest and easiest way out of a minor traffic infraction. If you are caught breaking a rule (inadvertently, of course), I suggest you listen with great patience to the horror of your crime and express true regret. Usually, this will result in a smile and a pleasant, "Be on your way and sin no more." However, if it appears this is not to be the case, I might ask "Can I pay the fine here?" or "How can I solve this problem without causing delay?" This will result in the exchange of a few pesos and everyone will depart as friends. Not only will you have saved yourself a lot of time and trouble, the experience will make for a great story when you return home. I must caution you, however, to *use your judgement!* If you are involved in a more serious situation (one involving injury to a person, for instance), do not, under any circumstances, offer a *mordida*. Instead, use your Mexican insurance policy as your shield.

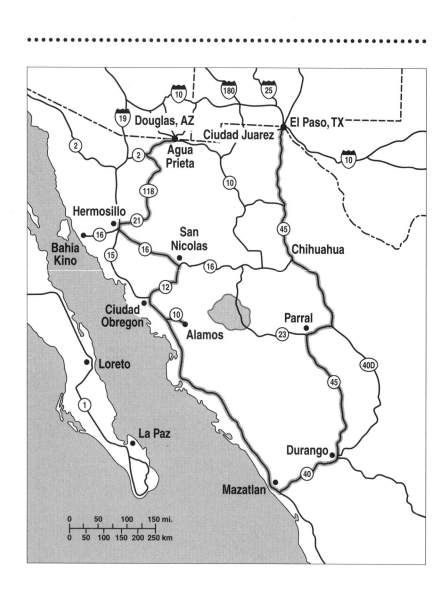

4 Missions, Mountains, Mazatlan, and More

This route begins in Douglas, Arizona, and follows the original trail of the *conquistadors* and Jesuit priests for a beautiful ride dotted with 17th-century missions, then it twists and turns through the high and desolate Sierra Madre Occidental to stop in Alamos, a town that is a national monument. From that point, we will make a dash to the Pearl of the Pacific: Mazatlan. The return trip will be via one of the most dramatic mountain roads in the world; some of the movie sets which were built to film Westerns in this area are still standing. A stopover at the site of Pancho Villa's last stand will complete the journey before you return to the U.S. at El Paso, Texas.

This route is approximately 3,000 km (1,870 mi.) and can be completed in seven days of riding. To enjoy the sights along the way and a day or two on the beach, plan on a minimum of twelve to fourteen days, but options are given to shorten this should you wish. Also, consider connecting to the beautiful Copper Canyon, a great experience that will only extend your driving by one day.

4.1 Douglas, Arizona to Hermosillo

Distance   *480 km (280 mi.)*

Features   *A fairly straightforward ride on good roads which follow the original route of the conquistadors and Jesuit priests. You'll encounter beautiful mountain riding and missions galore before arriving in the city of Hermosillo.*

Douglas, Arizona, rests on the Mexican border approximately 130 km (78 mi.) south of Interstate 10. From the west, take Exit 304 and head south on Hwy. 80. From the east, take Exit 5 south, which is also Hwy. 80 south.

Douglas is a fairly small city (pop. 13,000) with little of interest to the traveler. However, it has a very pleasant surprise in the **Hotel Gadsden,** 1046 G Ave. ($40; tel. 520-364-4481). This hotel was rebuilt in 1907 after a fire and is now a national historic site. The public areas are beautiful, with an Italian marble grand staircase, faux marble columns throughout the main lobby, and Tiffany stained glass murals. Be sure

You will be made to feel quite welcome when you enter Mexico. (Photo by Judy Kennedy)

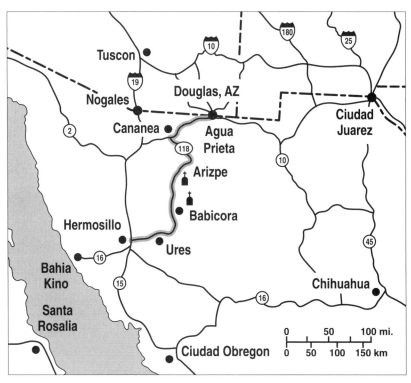

and go up to the mezzanine level where interesting photos and displays show the early history of the hotel and surrounding area. **Pancho Villa** rode his horse up the marble staircase and a hoofprint can still be found on the stairs. A ghost is said to visit single women in the middle of the night—but no complaints have been filed! The restaurant is more than adequate and maybe you can join the local domino game in the lobby. The rooms are basic but fully functional.

A simple, and usually timely border crossing at **Agua Prieta** will start the day. After completing the necessary paperwork, go straight on the main street to a T-intersection where you will turn left and then go right at the first traffic light. You will soon approach another T-intersection with Hwy. 2; the right turn will be clearly marked toward Cananea.

After approximately 90 km (56 mi.) of mostly flat, desert driving, you will come to a left turn that is marked ARIZPE, HWY. 89. (This may show as Hwy. 118 on your map, but the

A vado is a good place to wash a truck.

road is signed as Hwy. 89.) About 50 km (30 mi.) down this road, your entry papers will be checked.

The 220 km (136 mi.) from Cananea to Mazocahui is an up-and-down, twisting, curving road that has several *vados.* One or two may be slightly wet, but should present no problem to a bike except, perhaps, after a heavy rain. Expect the road surface to be generally very good. Vistas often show dramatic views of the river valley below, as you prepare to ascend and descend again and again. You will pass through several small villages that have **mission churches** founded by the Jesuits during the 17th century. Most are carefully maintained and still in use today. Photo opportunities abound! If you only have time to visit one church, I would recommend the one in **Babicora,** located right on the main square as you pass through town. The old mission is located beside the "new" cathedral which offers a unique contrast.

At the T-intersection with Hwy. 14 in **Mazocahui,** turn right and look forward to the final, startling descent through a boulder-filled canyon into **Ures.** From that point, the remaining miles run through flat desert to intersect with Hwy. 15, a four-laner just north of Hermosillo.

Follow Hwy. 15 south for approximately 20 km (12 mi.) and you will enter **Hermosillo.** Soon you will encounter an intersection where a left turn onto Hwy. 15 heads to Guaymas and straight ahead goes to the *centro.* Go straight ahead for three or so blocks and you'll find the Hotel Bugambilla on your right.

The **Hotel Bugambilla,** Blvd. Kino 712 ($45, includes breakfast; tel. 62-14-52-52) is on the main road through town. It has pleasant grounds with lots of green. The trees and flowers give it a tropical, Mexican feel. As you have your breakfast on the beautiful patio, the sounds of the birds in the trees will make for a very pleasant start to your day. I usually ask for one of the motel-type units where I can park my bike at the door. However, the newer high-rise unit next door does have nicer rooms, as well as a pool. The restaurant is very good and popular with the locals. Parking is secure in the lot provided.

Hermosillo is a modern Mexican city of over 700,000 people with a hidden, but still throbbing, colonial heart. You can get a good panoramic view of the city and the surrounding area from the **Cerro del la Campana** (Hill of the Bell).

The **Plaza Zaragoza,** located at the intersection of Blvds. Hidalgo and Rosales, is a nice shady setting in the midst of all the hustle and bustle. It is bordered by two of the cities main sights. The **Cathedral of the Assumption,** with its impres-

The original mission in Babicora has since been "replaced" by a new cathedral.

Three good reasons to slow down around blind curves.

sive white facade, sits on one end of the plaza. It was completed in 1908 to replace the original chapel constructed in 1778. It is a wonderful photo opportunity and well worth a visit. The **Palacio de Gobierno** holds down the other end of the plaza with its gray and white mass. Inside, a pleasant, tree-filled courtyard has colorful murals depicting area history.

As you would expect in any city of this size, supplies and services are abundant. For reliable, helpful, friendly motorcycle repair, seek out **Yamaval Motos,** S.A., Periferico Pte. and Ave. Santa Fe S/N (tel. 18-25-08).

Side Trip If you just can't wait to get to the beach and want to see an authentic Mexican fishing village, try a trip out to **Bahia Kino.** Just follow Hwy. 15 in Hermosillo until it intersects with Hwy. 16, which is clearly marked to Bahia Kino (110 km or 66 mi.). The drive will be straight and flat, with a few small towns containing interesting open-air markets along the sides of the road. Beware of people walking along the roadside, especially on weekends and *fiesta* days.

Bahia Kino is really two very separate and distinct villages. **Kino Viejo** (old) is what you will see as you first approach the sea. Its one paved street off to your left leads to the beach and the local boat launch. A ride down this divided street is like stepping into Mexico of 50 years ago. A little jaunt into and out of old Kino is well worth it. **Kino Nuevo** (new) is where the rich Americans and Mexicans build their beautiful condominiums. It is well developed along the bay and beach. For a wonderful experience, sit in a thatch-roofed, open-air restaurant eating fresh seafood while you watch the sun set behind a multitude of small, dramatic islands out in the **Sea of Cortez.**

The **Hotel Posada del Mar** ($30; tel. 624-2-01-55), located about halfway between the two towns, is probably the best place to stay. Be prepared with your own bottle of water, however. The place does overcome its shortage of amenities with its beautiful patio, walkways, and swimming pool. You can park your bike in the lobby.

If you get an early start and don't encounter problems or undue delays, it is possible to reach Bahia Kino in one day from Douglas, but the sun will be low on the horizon as you arrive. If there's any doubt, stay in Hermosillo and make this a day trip—or grab it on your way back. ■

Although some are in disrepair, most of the missions along this route are still in use today.

4.2 Hermosillo to Ciudad Obregon

Distance   *390 km (240 mi.)*

Features   *Be prepared for some rugged, remote mountain driving today. Carry plenty of water and some snack food, as reliable services will be few and far between. The overall distance is not that long, but the surface of these twisty mountain back roads will require you to drive at less than a normal pace. Be assured that you will encounter every road hazard to be found in Mexico on this beautiful ride: burros, potholes, cattle, diesel fuel spills—and anything else you can think of!*

As you depart the Hotel Bugambilla in Hermosillo, you must turn right and then U-turn to retrace your route to the intersection where Hwy. 15 to Nogales is straight ahead. Turn right here to get on the bypass toward Guaymas. Please note that there is no sign indicating this turn. Continue on this road until you see the left turn onto Hwy. 16 toward Chihuahua.

Mountain roads like this make a rider's wrist want to twist.

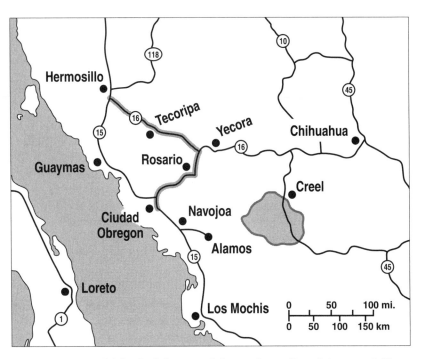

Make the left turn and then an immediate right to catch Hwy. 16. This is the easiest way out of town.

Should you wish to see **downtown Hermosillo,** turn right out of the hotel and follow the *centro* signs, and then pick up Hwy. 15 toward Guaymas. Watch for a left turn just as you are departing town. If you get to the desert you have gone too far. The sign is somewhat confusing, in that Hwy. 15 goes both straight and also to the left, as it splits into both toll and free highways. You want to take the left toward Santa Anna.

After approximately 2 km (1 mi.), take the right at the Y in the road onto Hwy. 16 toward P. Industrial. Then, at a T-intersection, turn right onto Hwy. 16 toward Chihuahua. After approximately 40 km (24 mi.) of straight, flat road through the desert, you will reach the town of **Colorada** where you will start to climb into the mountains.

Approximately 126 km (78 mi.) from Hermosillo you will come to the town of **Tecoripa.** Note that the PEMEX station on the highway as you're leaving town will be your last reliable chance for gas for the next 260 km (162 mi.) This will also be your last reliable chance to stock up on food and water for the

Churches dominate even the smallest of villages.

same distance. I would also suggest you spend some time flexing your left ankle to prepare for the sort of multiple shifting you'll be doing along this route.

After approximately 102 km (64 mi.) of some of the best riding you've ever had, you will reach a Y in the road. The road to the left is the continuation of Hwy. 16 leading to Chihuahua; the road straight ahead is unnumbered, but the sign indicates CIUDAD OBREGON. You want the unnumbered road straight ahead. Do not be confused by the left turn on Hwy. 117 just a mile or two before this intersection.

Connect   Should you wish to connect to the **Copper Canyon** instead of continuing to Mazatlan, take Hwy. 16 and after approximately 145 km (90 mi.) of mountain driving you will end up at **Basaseachic Falls.** From this point, see Chapter 5: The Copper Canyon. Gasoline is usually available in **Yecora** approximately 60 km (36 mi.) from this intersection. ∎

The road surface to this point should have been fair-to-good. The next 50 km (30 mi.) or so was fair-to-poor the last time I was there. It is not difficult, but it does require your reducing your speed to dodge potholes. After this stretch, the road once again improves. Enjoy the ride through this wild and mountainous outback. Traffic will be light and you will probably encounter more burros and horses than motorized vehicles.

You will leave the mountains behind and be back in the desert as you approach the town of **Rosario.** I am told that you may be able to find gasoline here. It was not available the last time I was through.

Turn right at a T-intersection, heading toward Esperanza, and continue until a left turn to Hornos intersects the main highway. Gasoline and all other services will be available here. Be cautious: this is not a rural road, but a four-lane highway with a strip of land with trees and bushes between opposite directions of travel! Although the sign indicates a left turn to Ciudad Obregon, this would put you into a lane of oncoming traffic. Instead, turn right and then U-turn into the other lanes at your first opportunity.

After a few miles, the road will intersect with Hwy. 15 south toward Ciudad Obregon. **Ciudad Obregon** offers all tourist facilities, a fact made all the more plain by the signs you'll see as you enter the city which indicate the *centro* straight ahead and a Wal-Mart to the right. The city can make for a pleasant overnight stop after a long day in the mountains, as all the major hotel chains will be represented. At the north end of town, The **Hotel Valle del Yaqui** (tel. 3-39-69) is a good choice, as is the **Holiday Inn.**

Ciudad Obregon was established when a railroad station was constructed at this location in 1921. Later, the damming of the **Yaqui River** converted hundreds of thousands of acres of arid desert into fertile farmland. As a result, Obregon has become a major agricultural area and one of the wealthiest towns in Mexico, even if it does lack interesting cultural and historical sights.

There are dual-sport opportunities around every bend in Mexico. (Photo by John Neff)

4.3 Ciudad Obregon to Alamos

Distance   *120 km (76 mi.)*

Features   *This is a short ride to the town of Alamos, most of which is via good, high-quality road. This day is designed to allow you to get to Alamos before lunch so you can enjoy a restful day in this lovely, historic town.*

Continue directly through Ciudad Obregon on Hwy. 15. Soon you will have to pay a 36-peso toll to continue to **Navajoa,** where the left turn to Alamos will be clearly marked. From Navajoa, the 50 km (30 mi.) to Alamos is mostly straight, flat, and narrow, with a dense growth of vegetation on each side of the road.

In **Alamos,** take a right at the Y as you enter downtown to arrive at the *plaza de armas.* The **Hotel Los Portales** ($30; tel 642-8-02-01), located on the plaza, is a converted colonial house that is clean and has all the basic amenities. The friendly family and staff that own and operate this small inn

This especially beautiful bandstand in the plaza de armas will likely offer a full night of free entertainment.

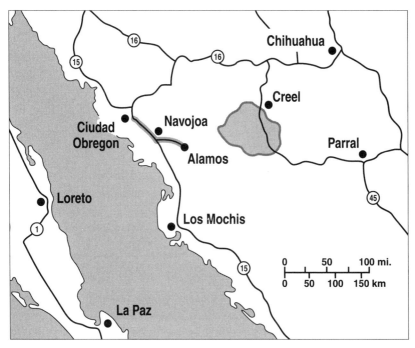

will make you feel right at home and make every effort to please. The rooms surround a small courtyard rich in greenery where you can park your bike just outside your room. The ride into the courtyard is rather exciting, however, as you have to ride your motorcycle up a ramp at the end of the block and through several small restaurants as you make your way down the portico. From there, you have to make a tight left turn through the narrow 17th-century door to get into the hotel.

Alamos, a declared **national monument,** is one of the gems of Mexico. The town came into being soon after discovery of silver nearby in 1683. It grew and flourished during the 1700s to a population once estimated at more than 30,000, and it had all the attractions of prosperous mining towns of the day, including its own mint. The silver slowly ran out and continued raids during the **War of Revolution** in the early 1900s nearly doomed it to fade away as just another town who had seen better days. During the late 1940s, however, it was "discovered" by American artists and a revival began.

Alamos is now a quiet little place with a great American influence and a population of approximately 6,000. It is one of the cleanest towns in Mexico and the residents are very proud of this fact, and work hard at maintaining its reputation. Many of the colonial *haciendas* in the town are now owned by Americans and have been restored to their former opulence. If you wish to visit a "typical" Mexican village from the 19th century, this is your place. It is filled with friendly folks who are very tolerant of *gringo* visitors.

The center of activity in Alamos is the *plaza de armas,* where you'll find the large stone church **La Parroquia de la Oyrusuna Concepcion,** as well as an almost mandatory wrought-iron kiosk which provides musical entertainment.

Lunch stop.

The jail in Alamos has a great view of the town below. (Courtesy of Pancho Villa Moto-Tours)

The plaza contains towering palm trees and is surrounded by restored buildings serving as hotels, museums, and restaurants. Walking tours of this town are well worth the few dollars they cost. **Jose "Candy Joe" Trinidar,** who can be found at his shop on the plaza, will gladly serve as your guide. You will be shown inside several *haciendas,* the cathedral, and the six-cell jail located on a hill overlooking the city.

4.4 Alamos to Mazatlan

∙∙

Distance   *600 km (370 mi.)*

Features   *The object today is to get to the beaches and fun of Mazatlan. Except for the return trip to Hwy. 15 in Navajoa, expect a straightforward, high-speed, mostly flat, four-lane road. Be prepared to spend approximately $20 on tolls. It is well worth the money, since the* libre, *while free, is slow, and there is nothing of real interest along the route. With a reasonably early start, you should arrive in Mazatlan by mid-afternoon.*

From Navajoa, follow the *cuota* south to Mazatlan. About 20 km (12 mi.) after the last toll plaza, look for a small sign indicating Mazatlan Playas; it is easy to miss. Take this exit to the right, following a two-lane road until it intersects with the large four-lane boulevard heading south into the hotel district known as the **Zona Dorado** (Gold Zone), which is filled with all types and prices of accommodations. You'll want to go left at this intersection, but first must go right around the round-about. This road continues south for about 11 km (7 mi.) before meeting the ocean at **Valentino's** disco, a large, white, Moorish-looking structure.

Your choice of hotels in **Mazatlan** will be unlimited. Obviously, the rooms on the beach will be pricier than the same

The beaches of Mazatlan offer sun, sea, and the opportunity to purchase souvenirs.

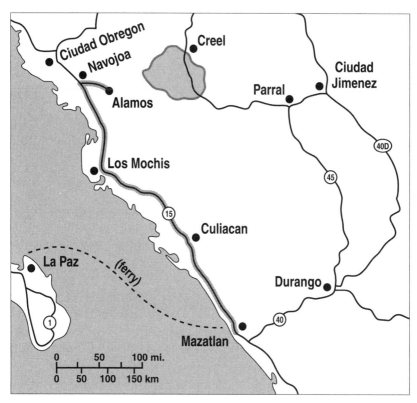

rooms across the street. My personal favorite is the **Playa Mazatlan,** Ave. Rodolfo T. Loaiza 202 (U.S. tel. 800-762-5816). The rack rates for the rooms are about $75 U.S. for the non-ocean view or $85 U.S. for an ocean view. (You came to Mazatlan to enjoy the beach, why not be on it!) These prices can be negotiable if the place isn't near full. I have paid as little as $50 U.S. for an ocean view room. Ask before you sign. It can't hurt, and you will not be charged more than the rack rate!

To get to the Playa Mazatlan, turn right off the main boulevard just before Valentino's. If you find the ocean on your right and no hotels, you've gone too far and should go back about one block up a one-way street on the left. They have comfortable rooms with all the amenities and a nice restaurant overlooking the bay. Arriving on a motorcycle will put you out of the mainstream of the hotel's guests and you may draw a crowd as you arrive. Directly across the street, the

Taxis,
Mazatlan-style.

Azteca Inn and **Plaza Gaviotas** can provide clean, comfortable, and less expensive accommodations.

Mazatlan, a city of approximately 600,000 people, is the northernmost of Mexican **beach resorts.** It is unique, in that it has not only a resort atmosphere and port activity, but also a thriving fishing industry, and a rich history. There are actually two Mazatlans, the **Zona Dorado** in the north, which is filled with hotels, discos, and everything a *gringo* tourist can imagine, and the southern portion, **the "old" city,** where you'll find business, history, and local inhabitants. These two very distinct areas are connected via a beautiful oceanside boulevard that seems to change name every other block.

Mazatlan, originally a small Indian settlement, became a **major port** for the Spanish in the 17th century. With the discovery of **gold and silver** in the Sierra Madre Occidental, it grew to be the primary port of export for bullion, and ships regularly returned filled with goods from Europe and Asia, prompting frequent raids by **pirates.** When mine production and Spanish influence decreased, the city declined but continued to be an important port. A rail link to the interior completed in the late 1800s helped the fishing industry, as it did other activity in the port. In the late 1950s, **American fishermen** "discovered" Mazatlan, and their stories of beautiful beaches, a mild climate, and friendly people quickly made it a favorite destination for tourists. Today **tourism** is Mazatlan's second most important industry, attracting a quieter crowd than many of the newer resorts. Many of the visitors return year after year.

The best view of Mazatlan is from the hill at the south end of town, where **El Faro,** the second-highest lighthouse in the world, has guided mariners to a safe haven for centuries. The **Basilica de la Immaculada Concepcion,** located on the Plaza Republicana at Juarez and 21 de Marzo, is at the center of the old city. While not very impressive on the outside, the interior, with its gilded baroque altar, is worth seeing. The **Plaza Republicana** is a pleasant place with the typical bandstand and shoe shine stands. These stands will not only shine your shoes, they also offer full-service repairs.

Much of the colonial architecture that still exists in the surrounding area is within a short walk of the plaza. The population is very proud of this area and major efforts are being made to renovate it. This effort is most evident at the **Plazuela Machado** located at Aves. Constitucion and Carnaval. The nearby **Teatro Angela Peralta,** which was

---

La Semana de la Moto

During late April or early May of each year, Mazatlan holds an equivalent of Daytona's Bike Week. This event will be in its fifth year in 2000 and it becomes bigger and better each year. Several blocks are barricaded off near the Plaza Mazatlan in the Zona Dorado and used exclusively for parking bikes. From Friday evening until a farewell on the following Tuesday morning, all types of activities are offered, including a parade through old Mazatlan, awards for various categories, races, events, meals, cocktail parties, and more. While it currently leans fairly heavily toward sport bikes, all types of motorcycles and motorcyclists are welcome. As in Daytona, a large part of the fun is strolling and inspecting the bikes, meeting new people, and exchanging viewpoints on the sport. Be assured that as an American tourer, you will be more than welcome. While this event has a way to go before it will approach the sheer numbers of Daytona, the gusto and friendliness cannot be matched. For more information, contact: Moto Club Mazatlan, Ave. Insurgentes #423, Fracc. Flamingos, Mazatlan Sin., Mexico, (tel. 69-86-06-24 or 16-54-14; e-mail igartua@sin1.telmex.net.mx). ■

built in the late 1800s in the grand Italian style, has since been completely restored and is now open daily to visitors for a small fee. A visit to the nearby central market can also give you a real look at the local lifestyle. The building has existed since 1895 and still is the major shopping area for city residents. The **Plazuela Zaragoza,** famous for its flower vendors, is the place to get a present for your lady. Also, the **aquarium** in Mazatlan, well known for its excellent collections, is located about midway on the oceanfront boulevard that connects the two portions of the city. Many visitors to Mazatlan never leave the Gold Zone and the beaches. A day spent exploring the old city during your stay will be well worth it.

Options   From Mazatlan you have some interesting choices:

- Return to **Nogales** via Hwy. 15, approximately 1,250 km (775 mi.), stopping over in any of the main cities along the road. Services will be good and plentiful. Consider spending a night in **Alamos** or **Bahia Kino** if you missed them on your way down.

- Take the **overnight ferry** from Mazatlan to **La Paz** and return to the U.S., as detailed in Clement

The Pearl of the Pacific—Mazatlan. (Photo by Lavoe Davis)

Ah, the beauties of Mexico! (Courtesy of Pancho Villa Moto-Tours)

Salvadori's book *Motorcycle Journeys Through Baja.* The ferry (tel. 69-81-20) leaves every day at 3 p.m. and arrives in La Paz 18 hours later. Your hotel should be able to give you current sailing times and rates. I would suggest visiting the ferry office the afternoon before you plan to travel, to confirm these numbers and reserve a stateroom. With a private stateroom, bath, and a motorcycle, plan on $100 fare, but this may change, so please verify beforehand.

- Continue on the route to **Durango,** returning to the U.S. at El Paso, Texas.

4.5 Mazatlan to Durango

Distance   *330 km (206 mi.)*

Features   *This is one of the best rides in Mexico—maybe in the world. Hwy. 40, one of the few east-west roads over the Sierra Madre Occidental, begins just south of Mazatlan at Villa Union and climbs to almost 9,000 feet, twisting and turning through tropical areas into high pine forests for more than 330 km (206 mi.), before descending into the beautiful colonial town of Durango. For very good reason, a portion of this road is known as El Espinazo del Diablo (The Devil's Backbone).*

Getting to Hwy. 15 south out of Mazatlan can be somewhat confusing. I have found the best way is to get directions to the *aeropuerto* from the hotel and then follow the signs. About 7 km (4 mi.) south of the airport, the left turn onto Hwy. 40 will be clearly marked. From that point, it is just a straightforward trek to Durango, but plan on stopping often for photographs

As you approach El Salto, the jungle lushness turns to high mountain pine forests with endless views. (Photo by Lavoe Davis)

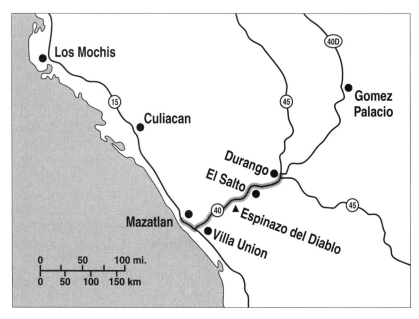

and sightseeing, as this route will have your eyes popping out of your head!

The two *vados* on the early portion of this route will present no problem unless there have been heavy rains recently. The truck traffic along this route can present some excitement, however, especially when you are going uphill and the truck is traveling downhill. These vehicles cannot make hairpin turns without entering your lane, and you will need to stay alert and be prepared to move to the edge of the pavement to give them room.

Although there are several small towns along this route, I would suggest you fill your tank prior to starting, as gasoline is not always available (just past the town of El Salto is your best bet).

Approximately 50 km (33 mi.) after leaving Mazatlan, Hwy. 40 passes through the town of **Concordia,** which is famous for its furniture making. Off the main highway, in the old town itself, a huge rocking chair in the main plaza celebrates their claim to fame.

Located approximately 100 km (62 mi.) before Durango, the high, remote town of **El Salto** offers great insight into the economy of this area. A raw and rugged logging town situated in dense pine forest at an altitude of more than 8,300 feet, El Salto feels like a real frontier town. If you love "getting away from it all" and back to nature, this is the place for you. The road flattens out and becomes straighter after El Salto.

It is fairly easy to reach the *plaza de armas* in Durango by merely following the signs for the zona centro. For a good shortcut, enter the city on the main road and look for the towers of the cathedral ahead in the distance. The road will then jog to the left. Constitution Street, on your right (the sign is on the building) will lead you directly to the plaza de armas. If you should miss this turn, continue following the centro signs until you intersect with the street 20 de Noviembre. From here, turn right and continue to the plaza. I recommend the **Hotel Posada San Jorge**, Constitucion #102 Sur, in Durango ($30; tel. 18-13-3257). It is a small, colonial-style hotel with upstairs rooms surrounding a courtyard. Secure

A beautiful day, great vistas, and a good road will make the drive from Mazatlan to Durango a delight. (Photo by Lavoe Davis)

A "local" inspects the gringo motorcycle.

parking is available only two blocks away. It is within one block of the *plaza de armas* and it has an excellent restaurant.

Durango, a city with a population of approximately 450,000, will give a false impression as you approach. The outskirts are modern and very industrial, but the center core is a colonial jewel. Durango was founded in 1523 by the Spaniards, but real occupation and construction didn't begin until the mid-1600s, due to its remote location and trouble with Indians. With the completion of a rail link to Mexico City in the early 1900s, Durango became an important point of transfer for timber harvested in the nearby mountains. It remains so today.

To fully appreciate the colonial influence and sights of the city, explore the area surrounding the *plaza de armas* on foot. Today, it contains wonderful architectural memories of the early days. Don't miss a visit to the **Cathedral de Durango** located at Ave. 20 de Noviembre on the main square. Churches on this site date back to 1571, but the current building was constructed between 1691 and 1770, and it towers over the square in its majesty. Inside there is a rare clerical pew from 1737 that is one of only two of its type to be found

A scene right out of a spaghetti western. (Photo by Dwight Carlos Hughes)

Twists, curves, and 1,000-foot drop-offs make this road well deserving of the name, "The Devil's Backbone." (Photo by Lavoe Davis)

in Mexico, as well as a collection of paintings from the 1600s depicting bishops. Other interesting sites within walking distance of the main square include the **Casa del Conde Suchil and Templo del Sagrado Corazon.**

The mountain which towers over the city of Durango, **Cerro de Mercado,** contains one of the largest iron ore deposits in the world. Mining has been underway there since the early 1800s and it is estimated that the reserves will last yet another 100 years. This mining activity, the timbering in the nearby pine forests, and the city's role as a hub of both rail and road transport continue to affect Durango's importance and growth.

Since the 1950s, Durango has been the site for the shooting of more than 100 **Western films.** The beautiful surrounding countryside will certainly revive memories of many of your old favorites. Should you wish, you can visit some of the old stage sets. The town of **Chupaderos,** located north on Hwy. 45 at km 14, is unusual in that it was built to represent an Old West town, but is now a going concern with Mexican squatters occupying the set buildings. Other sets, some occupied and some abandoned and rotting away, are popular tourist visits. Ask at the tourist office or your hotel and visit the one that perks your interest most.

By the way, all supplies and services should be readily available in Durango.

4.6 Durango to Chihuahua

Distance   *700 km (430 mi.)*

Features   *This day is a very nice, but rather long ride on a good main road. The high mountain and desert scenery will have you stopping often for photographs. Services should be plentiful. Should this prove too long a day, consider staying overnight in Parral and possibly doing a little sightseeing before continuing the next day.*

From the *plaza de armas* continue east on Ave. 20 de Noviembre for several blocks to the clearly-marked left turn onto Hwy. 45 to Parral. Expect this main highway to be in good condition, with great rolling hills and curves for the first 200 km (120 mi.) The wonderful mountain vistas on both

This old caballero now spends his days watching the world go by. (Photo by Dwight Carlos Hughes)

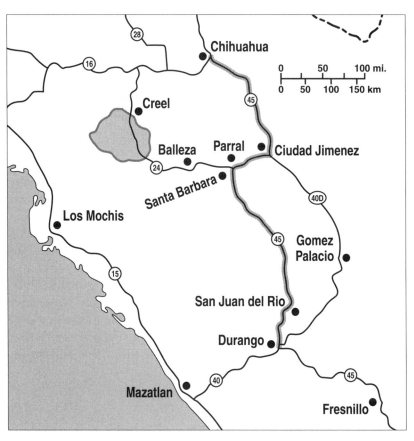

sides will remind you of the Old West you've seen in grade B movies from the 50s. I expect to see John Wayne around every curve.

From here, the road then flattens and straightens through scrubby, high desert pastureland before again turning into curves and twisties. As you approach Parral, a right turn will indicate Hwy. 45 toward Chihuahua. If you are continuing on to Chihuahua, take this turn and follow signs into the city. If you wish to overnight in Parral, continue straight down the pleasant, divided boulevard lined with palm trees, and on your left you will find the adequate **Motel Camino Real,** Ave. Independencia S/N (tel. 3-02-02).

Parral, a bustling, prosperous town with an old town history, originally came to exist as a result of the mining in the area. Since initial discovery at the **La Nignita** mine in 1631,

Parral saw more than 200 other mines come and go, until falling prices and a decline in the richness of the ores made it uneconomical in the early 1980s. The decline of the mines has since been offset by the building of a General Motors auto plant and an increase in farming in the area.

Parral contains several interesting plazas, old churches, and buildings within its narrow streets. Today, it claims fame as the location where **Pancho Villa** was killed and originally buried (see sidebar). A small museum, **Museo de General Francisco Villa,** has several interesting displays detailing Villa's life and death. Ask for directions to find the plaque that marks the spot where he was killed.

It is very hard to get around in Parral, as the roads twist and turn, crossing the river more than nine times in the downtown area. I suggest you get a motel near the center of town and use a taxi for your sightseeing. Among the sights is the **Catedral de San Jose,** which was built with mining money and now contains the remains of **Don Juan Rangel de Viesma,** Parral's founder. Pieces of ores from nearby mines decorate the pillars that support the roof. The nearby **Palacio**

Pancho Villa, the original "outlaw" biker, actually did consider mounting his men on iron horses. (Photo courtesy of the El Paso Public Library)

Francisco "Pancho" Villa

So many legends exist regarding the exploits of Pancho Villa that it is difficult to determine fact from fiction. You can be sure, however, that he is still a hero to the poor people of Mexico and any comment by a *gringo* degrading his name or actions will be met with hostility.

Born about 1879 in San Juan del Rio as Doroteo Arango, little is known of Villa's early years, but he was of the peasant class and life must have been hard indeed. At the age of 16, he killed a man in Durango for allegedly molesting one of his sisters. From this time on he lived a life of crime, and by the age of 20 he had added cattle stealing and bank robbery to the list of crimes for which he was wanted. From 1900 until 1910, he and his gang lived in the Sierra Madre Occidental and established a Robin Hood reputation with the locals, robbing and stealing at will, while always escaping the efforts of government troops *(rurales)* to capture them.

In 1910, Mexico's presidential election pitted the ruling capitalist party against the growing opposition of various groups looking for socialist reforms and help for the lower classes. The election was corrupt and revolution filled the air. Villa took this opportunity to come down from the mountains and join with other groups to form the Division del Norte. In this way, he transformed himself and his followers from *banditos* to *revolucionarios.*

Although Villa successfully liberated the states of Sonora and Chihuahua, he was not able to maintain a strong central government. It wasn't until 1916 that peace and order returned to the country, and that was only accomplished by the intervention of the U.S. government.

In 1919, Villa retired to Canutillo with his comrades, known as *dorados* (the golden ones). On July 20, 1923, while on a banking trip into Parral, seven riflemen pumped more than 150 bullets into his Dodge automobile. It has been rumored that they were hired by the government because Villa was too popular with the people. Over 30,000 people attended his funeral.

Even in death, Villa would cause controversy. Three years after he was buried in Parral, someone dug up the body and cut off the head, and it has never been found. Three years after this incident, the federal government ordered the body to be moved to a special tomb in Mexico City for heroes of the revolution. Local legend has it that the body was switched with one from an adjoining grave and the body now in Mexico City is not Villa's. ■

An excellent road through the mountains makes the ride from Parral to Creel a delight. (Photo by Dan Kennedy)

Alvarado, located at the corner of Calle P. de Verdad and Riva Palacio, was originally a hotel but was later given to Pancho Villa for his own use.

To continue on to Chihuahua, turn right before entering **Parral** on Hwy. 45. After approximately 80 km (50 mi.) of good, two-lane road, you will pick up a section of four-lane road. The road will alternate between two lanes and four lanes until you reach Chihuahua, but it is a good-surfaced, high-speed drive through high desert.

In **Chihuahua** and the surrounding area there are accommodations available in every price range. I recommend staying downtown near the *plaza de armas,* which allows walking access to all the main sights. The **Posada Tierra Blanca,** at Ave. Niños Heroes 102 ($60; tel.14-15-00-00) offers adequate accommodations with secure parking and is only a few blocks from the plaza. It has a startling mural in the lobby. As you approach from the south, follow the CENTRO signs until you arrive at the plaza. Consider using a taxi to guide you in for the last few blocks, as this is a very busy and confusing area.

Side Trip   For a delightful alternative, continue from Parral to **Creel** (200 km, 153 mi.) and on to the **Copper Canyon.** This is an all day drive and you will need to stop overnight in Creel before continuing. From your motel, turn right and retrace your route to the intersection with Hwy. 45, then turn right toward Santa Barbara. Soon you will need to take a left toward Santa Barbara onto a highway marked as 259. Should you come to the PEMEX facility, you have gone too far. From this point, you will come to a Y-intersection, where you will take a right onto Hwy. 24. Then just follow the signs to Creel. All services will be available in the town of Balleza.

As you come to a T-intersection, a right turn continues on to Creel. A left will take you into the main part of **Balleza.** This is a newly-paved road of curves, curves, and more curves. Also, it offers dramatic mountain scenery and very little traffic. From here, see Chapter 5 to continue. ■

A dual-sport rider has almost endless options in Mexico. (Courtesy of Pancho Villa Moto-Tours)

The city of **Chihuahua** is also the capital of the state by the same name. With a population exceeding 600,000, the city is typical of most larger Mexican towns, in that it is prosperous, busy, and modern, with a kernel of history in the center. The *plaza de armas* is where all the action takes place, and it has a delightful cathedral. The **Museum of Sacred Art** contains religious paintings and many items from the colonial period. The **Palacio de Gobierno** facing the **Plaza Hidalgo** has a courtyard whose walls are covered with murals showing the history of the area. Some of the more interesting sights are quite a walk, but taxis are inexpensive and will free you from the hassle of having to navigate on your own.

One sight worth visiting is the **Museo Regional** (Quinta Gameros). **Manuel Gameros** intended this mansion to be a wedding present for his soon-to-be-wife, but by the time it was completed she had fallen in love with the architect. He gave it to them as a wedding present. Today it is open to the public and its art nouveau decoration offers quite a contrast to other buildings in the area. One room upstairs is devoted to **Paquime artifacts** (see Nuevo Casas Grandes).

Originally founded by Spanish mining activity in 1718, Chihuahua proved to be a very difficult area to settle because of continued uprisings by the local Indians. Chihuahua has a rich history regarding the various struggles in Mexican history. During the War of Independence, Padre Miguel Hi-

Always plan on throwing your chain near a town or village.

The Dog by the Name of Chihuahua

Those small dogs with big ears and eyes are familiar to us all, especially since Taco Bell has featured one in its series of commercials. This eponymous breed was introduced to the U.S. from the area of Chihuahua, but how it came to be there is unknown, although stories abound. Today, this dog is in the minority in his "home" state, as the prevalent canine in northern Mexico is what is known as the *bastido mexicano.* For some reason, the chihuahuas you do see here are much larger than those typically seen in the States.   ■

dalgo, the **Father of Mexican Independence,** fled here. He was captured, imprisoned, subjected to questioning by the Holy Office of the Inquisition, and executed here in 1811. His **prison cell,** located underneath the Post Office on Juarez, has been made into a small museum displaying some of his personal effects.

In 1910, during the **Mexican Revolution,** Pancho Villa and his army took the city and made it his home and headquarters. He still is quite a hero in this city. Upon Villa's assassination in 1912, quite a battle developed regarding legal ownership of his property. It seems that he had a habit of getting married but not getting divorced! After a struggle between three former wives and at least twenty mistresses, his estate was awarded to **Luz Corral de Villa,** and is now known as Quinta Luz. Located at Calle 10 and Mendez, **Quinta Luz** has become one of the better museums depicting the life and times of Pancho Villa. In the courtyard sits the car in which Villa was riding when he was killed, bullet holes and all. It is a sight not to be missed. From the *plaza de armas,* take a taxi.

4.7 Chihuahua to El Paso, Texas

Distance   *370 km (230 mi.)*

Features   *Expect a day of good roads and high-speed highway, most of it four-lane divided.*

After departing your hotel, simply follow Hwy. 45 signs toward Juarez. Most of this high desert route has views for miles and miles. You'll encounter plenty of services (and trucks) along the way. You'll need to submit your exit papers at the entrance checkpoint well south of Juarez. To legally exit, you must U-turn at this checkpoint, enter Lane 4 heading south and turn in your decal and paperwork. Then, you will need to U-turn toward the north to exit Mexico. As you enter **Ciudad Juarez,** follow the signs for the **punte internacionale** (international bridge). Be prepared—this is a

Mexico offers new pleasures around every curve.

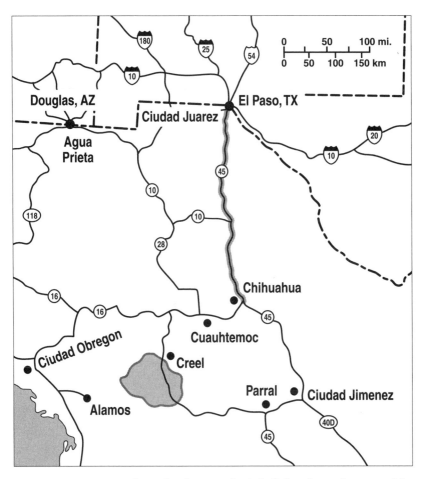

very busy border crossing! Splitting lanes is acceptable, however.

Connect   To connect to the **Copper Canyon** route from Chihuahua, follow the signs on Hwy. 16 toward Cuauhtemoc. After approximately 110 km (66 mi.) you can pick up the route to the Copper Canyon on Hwy. 16 shortly after passing through **Cuauhtemoc.**

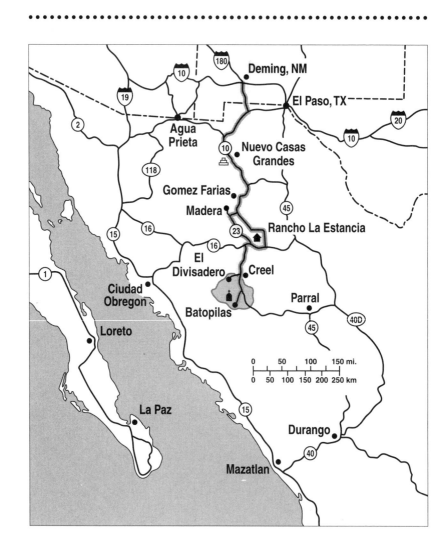

5 The Copper Canyon

This suggested route starts and ends in Deming, New Mexico, and will take you to one of the most remote areas of northern Mexico. The destination, Barranca de Cobre, is one of North America's most dramatic and least-known natural wonders. A series of canyons up to 6,000 feet deep form a natural depression estimated at four times the size of the Grand Canyon. On top of the natural beauty of the terrain, you will encounter the Tarahumara Indians, Mormon settlements, Mennonite farming communities, an almost deserted mining town, and some of Mexico at its best. The direct-driving distance is approximately 1,400 km (870 mi.) for which you should allow a minimum of five days of traveling and one day in the canyon. To enjoy the suggested side trips and stops, plan on a 2,100 km (1,300 mi.) trip of seven or eight days. To fully explore this area and all its wonders, plan on a lifetime of fun.

5.1 Deming, NM to Nuevo Casas Grandes

Distance   *250 km (157 mi.)*

Features   *The goal today will be to clear border formalities and get into the interior of Mexico. Expect a straightforward, short day on good-surfaced roads through the desert. There will be frequent gasoline stations and several good roadside restaurants.*

Deming, a small New Mexico town located at Exits 82/85 on I-10, has several national chain motels on the interstate which could serve as your base. The best local hotel is the **Grand Motor Inn** located on Motel Drive (tel. 505-546-2632). If you have trucked or trailered your bike, several local RV parks can store your unit for a small fee until you return. See Don Cameron, owner of **Deming Cycle Center,** 820 East Spruce (tel. 505-546-2193) for help solving those last-minute supply/repair problems. You will also find the ever-present Wal-Mart to cover your other last-minute needs.

From Deming, head south on Hwy. 11 through flat farmland. After 30 or so miles, you will enter the city of **Columbus,** New Mexico, a small, mostly deserted town noted as the only city in the United States ever to have been invaded by a foreign force (Pancho Villa, 1916). There is a **small museum** in town documenting the battle. Villa attacked in retaliation

Deming Cycle Center, in Deming, New Mexico, is good for last-minute repairs and supplies.

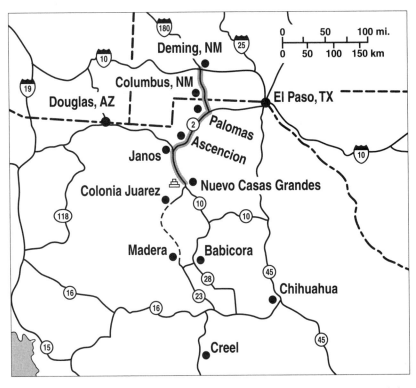

for the U.S. withdrawing its support from his cause and de-claring support for the Carranza presidential candidacy in Mexico. It is also rumored that he was aggravated that his last supply of ammunition from the U.S. Army was of the wrong caliber. Following Villa's raid on March 9, 1916, the U.S. Army, led by **General John Pershing,** traveled as far south as Parral in pursuit of Villa, but they never captured him.

Palomas is an easy border crossing into Mexico. It is mostly used to pass agricultural goods into the U.S. How-ever, be forewarned, while the crossing is open every day of the week, 24 hours a day, finding a copy machine (see en-trance requirements) may be a problem outside of normal business hours. As you approach the border, make a right turn just before the gateway into a gravel parking lot. Park your bike and walk over to obtain the necessary permits. Af-ter a quick inspection of your bike you will be on your way. The town of Palomas itself has little of interest. After clearing customs, I suggest you continue straight through town on Hwy. 24.

If you approach from the west, you could save some miles by crossing the border at **Agua Prieta-Douglas, Arizona** (see Chapter 4) and following Hwy. 2 east to the intersection with Hwy. 10 at Janos, and then pick up the rest of the route from there. If you approach from the east, I suggest you continue to Deming on I-10 rather than cross at **El Paso, Texas,** as you will save no mileage and can avoid the hassle of the busy El Paso crossing.

After clearing customs, follow Hwy. 24, a good, paved road through high desert, for approximately 30 km (18 mi.) to the T-intersection with Hwy. 2. Do not be fooled by the building at this intersection that appears to be a customs inspection station. It is abandoned. You will not be asked for your papers until south of Janos, almost 150 km (93 mi.) inside the border.

Turn right onto Hwy. 2 and continue through the desert for approximately 115 km (70 mi.) until you intersect with Hwy. 10 in Janos. From here, follow the signs to Nuevo Casas Grandes, 55 km (35 mi.). Up to this point you will have been

A dual-sport rider can explore endless back roads in Mexico. (Courtesy of Pancho Villa Moto-Tours)

on a very busy two-lane road with a good bit of truck traffic. After Janos this should ease. This entire route is in good condition and you should make excellent time, but do remember the general hazards of driving in Mexico and adjust your alertness accordingly.

Nuevo Casas Grandes, a town of 80,000 or so people, is a center of agriculture and trading. In the late 1800s, **Mormons** fleeing the new U.S. law prohibiting polygamy settled at eight locations in Mexico. During the revolution they returned to the U.S., but they returned to Mexico after the revolution; the Casas Grandes area is one of only two remaining settlements. The **modern farming** techniques they introduced here have had dramatic results, and growing fruit and making cheese are the main industries in the area. They even have their own packing company to ship their product to the U.S. and throughout Mexico.

For an interesting side trip, visit the Mormon settlement of **Colonia Juarez,** approximately 30 km (18 mi.) southwest of Nuevo Casas Grandes via Hwy. 18. These people are proud of their heritage and accomplishments and are more than willing to enlighten you as to the history and background of

A boy soon learns who his true friends are. (Courtesy of Mexico's Ministry of Tourism)

the area. Colonia Juarez has a bilingual school for grades one through twelve that provides graduates with certificates accepted both in Mexico and the U.S. Over 80 percent of its graduates continue on to college.

Nuevo Casas Grandes is prosperous and reminds me more of a southwestern U.S. town than of Mexico, but it is a good first night's stop, as all the necessary services will be available and there are some interesting side trips nearby. There is a bypass, but you will want to stay on the main highway marked CENTRO, which will put you on a wide avenue that runs through the center of town. In my opinion, the best hotel in town is the **Motel Hacienda** on the main drag, Ave. Juarez 2603 ($40; tel. 4-10-46; fax 4-48-18). The rooms are clean

They grow 'em big in Mexico.

The Paquime Ruins

The Paquime ruins represent all that remain of a civilization that existed for 700 years. The first people to practice agriculture in northwest Mexico, they were known to have been in existence as early as 700 C.E., and the influence of the Paquime probably peaked during the 12th century. Located on the banks of the river, their multi-story adobe city was the focal point of trading during the 11th and 12th centuries for the American southwest and southern Mexico. The size of these buildings are the origin of the town's name, Casas Grandes (big houses). The city was abandoned in the mid-1300s, possibly due to destruction by enemies from the north, and fire. Whatever the reason, the people left the city and where they went remains a mystery.

These complex structures not only had running water brought from springs to the north, but also a water refuse system to remove wastes. The multi-roomed, multi-storied buildings were fitted together in a jumble of angles and the rooms may have up to sixteen interior walls each. It appears these rooms were heated and many had exterior windows for ventilation. The doorways are of a T-shape that allow only one person at a time to pass, while still allowing for items to be carried through in the arms. It is believed this was done for defensive purposes. The excavated portions of the town include ball courts, military encampments, a platform for making offerings to the gods, and ceremonial plazas. A stone cross lying on the ground with its arms aligned with the points of the compass appears to have been used to predict the seasons.

To reach the Paquime ruins from Nuevos Casas Grandes, continue south, making a right turn toward Casas Grandes, and watch for a sign indicating the left turn to the ruins (approx. 10 km, or 6 mi.).   ■

and spacious, the staff is friendly and mostly bilingual, and the restaurant is good. It has a pool surrounded by a nice courtyard. If you ask for a room on the courtyard, you can park your bike by your door. The only drawback is that this hotel is also a popular tour bus stop. There are many other accommodations in this city, some of which are of equal value. Most are located on Ave. Juarez.

5.2 Nuevo Casas Grandes to Creel

Distance   *410 km (255 miles)*

Features   *This is a straightforward, good road, running mostly through high desert leading into high pine forest, before winding through the Sierra Madre Occidental and arriving in Creel.*

Follow Hwy. 10 south from Nuevo Casas Grandes for approximately 80 km (50 mi.) to the intersection with Hwy. 23 in **Buenaventura.** Turn right on Hwy. 23 toward Gomez Farias, and it will be an additional 330 km (205 mi.) to Creel. Hwy. 23 makes a right turn just after the town of **La Junta** at the PEMEX station. There will be a fairly good restaurant on the right after the turn, as well as a mini supermarket and liquor store. Gasoline, refreshments, food, and services will be readily available along this route.

After about 20 km (12 mi.) Hwy. 23 separates from Hwy. 16 with a left turn toward Creel. If you were to continue straight on Hwy. 16 for approximately 80 km (50 mi.), you'd be at **Casada de Basaseachic** (Basaseachic Falls), the third highest waterfall in North America at 1,000 feet. The park itself is pristine, with at least five other waterfalls, but outside the park, logging and overgrazing have eroded the natural beauty of the area. To view the falls, plan on a one-hour, round-trip walk to and from the viewpoint. If you wish to go

Need a little dual-sport time? (Photo by Dan Kennedy)

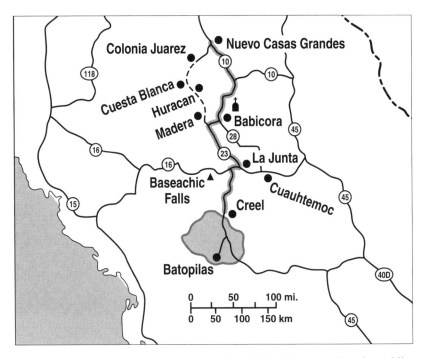

down to the bottom of the falls, plan on a three-hour hike (two hours uphill). If you take this side trip, add an additional four hours to your day.

Connect   To connect with the Chapter 4 route, continue west on Hwy. 16 past the falls for approximately 150 km (95 mi.) of increasingly beautiful mountain riding, until you intersect with the route near **San Nicolas.** I would recommend stopping for gasoline at **Yepachic,** as services are few and far between after that. Wonderful ride! ■

Options   An alternate route for those riding dual-sport bikes would be to take the road out of Nuevo Casas Grandes to Colonia Juarez and then proceed to **Madera** via improved dirt roads through magnificent high pine forest as remote as you would ever wish to get. The route is often confusing: Colonia Juarez to **San Diego** to **Cuesta Blanca** to **Huracan** (gas available) via dirt, then on to Madera. This is not a difficult road, but involves at least five water crossings and is criss-crossed with logging roads and roads to *estancias.* Take water and food, as there is none available along this 250 km (150 mi.) stretch, and plan on becoming lost and asking a local cattle herder for

This Tarahumara child has not yet learned to be shy. (Courtesy of Pancho Villa Moto-Tours)

directions to whatever the next town is. In spite of this, I found this to be a most delightful ride and would recommend it highly. ■

If you don't reach pavement in time to make Creel before dark, the **Hotel Real del Bosque** ($35; tel. 157-2-05-38) in the south of Madera is more than adequate for an overnight stay. When I was last in Madera, the water to the entire city was cut off from between the hours of 5 to 8 p.m. I never could find out why.

Placed in a valley at approximately 7,700 ft. in altitude and consisting of about 3,000 souls, **Creel** is primarily a logging town that is slowly turning into a tourist stop, as it is acknowledged as the jumping-off point for visiting the **Copper Canyon.** All services will be available in Creel: gasoline, hotels, laundry, restaurants, souvenir shops, and whatever else you might need. Overlooking the city from a nearby hill, there is a statue of Christ blessing the whole goings-on. The **Motel Parador de la Montaña** ($45; tel. 145-6-00-75), 41 Ave. Lopez Mateos, is the one I recommend. However, there are many alternatives. You will see **Tarahumara Indians** everywhere selling their works. They do not live in Creel, but

Tarahumara Indians

The actual name for these very secretive and quiet people is the Raramuri, which means "running people;" the name "Tarahumara" is the result of a corruption by the invading Spanish.

When the Spanish expanded into the area of central Chihuahua, the Tarahumara occupied the more fertile lands. As attempts to "civilize," enslave, or baptize them became more intense, they moved further into the rugged highlands of the Sierra Madre Occidental, a migration which continues even to this day. They are a people committed to continuing their own way of life, language, customs, and religion, even at the expense of modern-day comforts. Although they have been studied by many eminent scholars, no one has really ever been able to invade the culture and thinking of these people.

In Creel and Batopilas you will encounter Tarahumara selling their wares on the streets. They are extremely shy and won't look you in the eye. They do not live in these towns, but are semi-nomadic, living outside the towns in caves or stone huts and moving up and down the mountains according to the season. Do not ever presume to enter a Tarahumara home or take a photograph without first obtaining permission.

These "running people" have the amazing ability to run for days kicking a small wooden ball with their feet, covering 40–60 miles a day, depending on the terrain. It is also said that they can capture deer and other animals by running them to the point of exhaustion. In 1968 the Mexican government entered two Tarahumara in the 26-mile Olympic marathon, but they did not finish at the top. They maintained that the "shortness" of the race and the fact that they were forced to wear shoes, made it not worth the effort. Perhaps we should introduce a 60-mile, barefoot marathon.

To me, the most amazing thing about the Tarahumara has been their ability to maintain their culture through centuries of constant conflict. When you encounter these people, please respect their 400-year old commitment to maintain their privacy.   ■

in small settlements outside of town. They are very shy and will seldom look you in the eye, even when bargaining. Do not attempt to take their picture without asking permission first.

5.3 Exploring The Copper Canyon

Distance   *Your total distance will be approximately 260 km (160 mi.), including a steep, 40 km (24 mi.) dirt grade into and out of the Copper Canyon.*

Features   *The goal for the next two days is to see and explore this wonder of nature. I recommend an overnight stop in Batopilas.*

Batopilas, a town of approximately 600 people, rests in an oasis at the bottom of the canyon. It has a rich history as a mining town. When the Spanish arrived in Batopilas in 1634, they found pure silver rocks weighing up to 500 pounds along the banks of the river. At one time, Batopilas was one of the wealthiest towns in Mexico. In fact, it was the second town in Mexico to get electricity.

Eventually, the difficulty in getting ore out of the canyon and the expulsion of the Spanish in the 1820s brought a halt to the mining. However, it was resumed in the mid-1800s

The abundant views from the rim of the Copper Canyon will have you stopping often.
(Photo by Dan Kennedy)

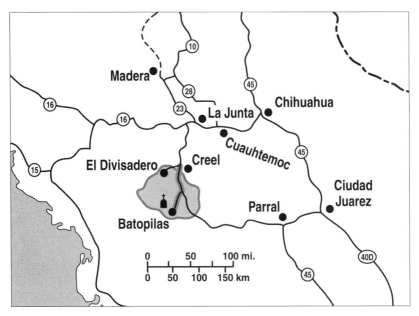

(see sidebar). Some gold and silver is still extracted by local independent miners, but the primary industry today is **growing marijuana,** as evidenced by the disproportionate number of high-priced SUVs parked on the streets next to the mules and horses. Batopilas is by no means a lawless or dangerous town. The locals mind their own business and a casual visitor will not be bothered by or even aware of the goings-on. If you ride your bike into Batopilas, however, expect to be inspected for drugs both going in and coming out.

Most of the buildings in Batopilas date from the mid-to-late 1800s and the town really has a flavor that should not be missed. I would suggest that you take some minimal food with you, as the restaurants and grocery stores seem to work on a schedule of their own. The **Hotel Mary** is the place to stay, and reservations can be made by calling a central booking agent ($20; tel. 15-54-08 or 10-45-80); the hotel itself has no phone. Be sure and request a room with bath. The facilities are clean and adequate, with a nice courtyard and restaurant. Several other facilities exist in town, primarily as guest rooms in private houses. The **Copper Canyon Riverside Lodge,** a restored *hacienda,* is the premier facility in town, but they require a minimum of seven nights' stay in conjunc-

Magnificent views and curving, descending dirt roads make for an exciting ride into the Copper Canyon.

Quite a ride ahead! (Photo by Dan Kennedy)

As you reach the bottom of the Copper Canyon, you will find the river that exposed vast lodes of silver.

tion with tours to other commonly-owned hotels. It is worth strolling in and wandering around, however.

In or nearby Batopilas are several other sights worth a visit:

- **Lost Cathedral:** This mission church is located approximately 7 km (4 mi.) south of town on the only road out, a good dirt road that can be easily handled by a dual-sport bike. Tour operators will surely include it as part of your itinerary. Alternately, you could hire a local truck to take you there and back, or you could (gasp) walk. The date of its founding and the early history of this church are a mystery. The bells have striking dates dating back to 1630, but there is no mention of this church in Vatican records. If the church was founded by Jesuits, later Franciscans may have destroyed their records. In any case, the local people have taken great pride in restoring this church to its former glory. Well worth the trip.

- **Hacienda San Miguel:** This is the former home and factory of Alexander Shepherd, the founder of the Batopilas Mining Company (see sidebar). The house,

The "lost" mission of Batopilas.

The ruins of Sheperd's home and foundry in Batopilas lead one to contemplate the rewards of this world

foundry, and associated facilities lie in ruins today, overgrown by the lush vegetation that proliferates in the area. It's a short walk to the ruins on the east side of the river. Recommended.

- **Aqueduct and power generating plant:** In the late 1800s, Shepherd not only built an aqueduct to provide water to the town, he also established a power generating plant. Although it has since been refurbished, this still provides the power source for the town. It is well worth the walk to the north of town, below the bridge, to see this engineering marvel still functioning.

The best way to get to Batopilas is by dual-sport bike. (I would not recommend the trip on a street bike.) From Creel, take Hwy. 23 south for about 70 km (42 mi.) to the clearly-marked right turn to Batopilas. It is a wonderful high moun-

Batopilas Mining Company

A great deal of what you see in Batopilas today is the result of one man, Alexander Shepherd, and his company, the Batopilas Mining Company. Unlike the absent owner who takes treasure out of an area and leaves nothing in return, Shepherd left behind a wonderful legacy.

Batopilas was a great source of silver for the Spanish, but when they were expelled in 1820 the mining stopped. Mexican companies resumed a small amount of mining in the 1840s, but their success was limited. Then an American, John Robinson, bought up some properties thought to be mined out in the early 1860s and discovered La Veta Grande (the Great Vein), a hereto unknown source. Robinson either did not realize the size of his discovery, or felt the cost of transporting ore to Chihuahua for processing was prohibitive, because he sold his holdings in Batopilas to another American, Alexander Shepherd, for the goodly sum of $600,000 in 1880.

Shepherd, whose tenure as governor of Washington, D.C., ended when Congress removed him from office for alleged corruption, moved to Batopilas, started buying up other outlying claims, and formed the Batopilas Mining Company. He solved the problem of transporting the ore by building his own refinery and foundry in his Hacienda San Miguel and instead, transported out refined, pure silver ingots. Often the monthly mule train would carry out up to 200 of these ingots, each weighing 70 pounds. Needless to say, Batopilas was one of the wealthiest spots in Mexico.

Shepherd and the wealth created by the Batopilas Mining Company created an incredible city in this remote canyon. Most of the fine homes still standing today were built during its heyday. Theater and the arts blossomed. The company built a viaduct and hydroelectric facility, only the second such in Mexico at the time; it is still the source of the town's electricity today. At its peak, the Batopilas Mining Company was one of the wealthiest companies in the world, paying over $1,000,000 in dividends per year.

Shepherd died in 1902 and the mines played out in the early 1920s, when Batopilas went into decline and the Company fell into oblivion— but, the city remains a jewel even today. ∎

tain road with sweepers, twisties, and a very good surface. There is a small grocery store at the turn-off for any last-minute supplies. It is hard to go wrong from here, as there is only one other road off to the right.

The first 30 km (18 mi.) or so is a hard-packed, mostly-level road meandering through the forest. Then the road begins the more than 6,000-foot descent into the canyon. This is not a technically difficult drive—buses and supply trucks make the trip every day—but it is rocky and steep at points and will require your attention. The views of the canyon will blow your mind; frequent photo stops are required. Please remember if the sun is wrong for a shot, you will be coming back the next day, as this is the only road in and out. After approximately 40 km (24 mi.) you will level off and cross the river bridge into Batopilas.

Alternatively, you could hire a four-wheel drive vehicle to take you into the canyon, typically for a two-day excursion with an overnight stay in the Hotel Mary or something equivalent. Some of these vehicles even have seats attached to the top so you can get an unimpaired view of the canyon during the descent—not for the faint of heart! Your hotel in Creel should be able to make the arrangements for you. Obviously you could save a few bucks by sharing this adventure with other similarly-minded travelers.

You can also get a super view of the canyon from **El Divisadero.** As you are going south on Hwy. 23, note the paved road on the right to San Rafael. This road will take you

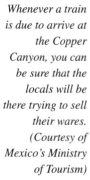

Whenever a train is due to arrive at the Copper Canyon, you can be sure that the locals will be there trying to sell their wares. (Courtesy of Mexico's Ministry of Tourism)

The beautiful Posada Barrancas Mirador offers spectacular views of the canyon and there are fireplaces in every room. The two-hundred dollar a night tariff includes three meals. Views aren't cheap.

through 50 km (30 mi.) of some of the best mountain riding I have ever encountered anywhere in the world. It is well-marked and the surface is good. The last half mile before arriving in El Divisadero was good hard-pack when I was last there, but it will probably be paved soon. If you really want a treat, stay at the **Hotel Posada Barrancas Mirador** (681-5-70-46). Every room has a view of the canyon, a sitting area outside the room, and a fireplace. The food is good, plentiful, and included in the room rate of approximately $200 per night.

The day following your visit to Batopilas you will ascend out of the canyon to Creel via the same route. For a final look into the canyon, take the side trip to El Divisadero I just described.

5.4 Creel to Rancho la Estancia

Distance   *200 km (120 mi.)*

Features   *After the thrills and rigors of the trip into and out of the canyon, this will give you a chance to sleep in and have a short day of good, paved road descending from the heights of Creel into lower flatlands. You'll go through some amazing Mennonite farming country to a wonderful, isolated, world-renowned fly-in hunting resort.*

Retrace your route up Hwy. 23 north out of Creel to the T-intersection with Hwy. 16 and take a right turn. At the next T-intersection (the one with the PEMEX station), turn right to continue on Hwy. 16 toward Cuauhtemoc. After riding approximately 170 km (100 mi.) from Creel, as you are approaching Cuauhtemoc, take a left onto Hwy. 65 toward Gomez Farias (just past the PEMEX station). After approximately 20 km (12 mi.), you'll see the well-marked dirt road on the left that leads to the Rancho.

An alternate method of exploring the Copper Canyon is a 4WD van. The couple riding on the roof may lose their fillings by the end of the day, however.

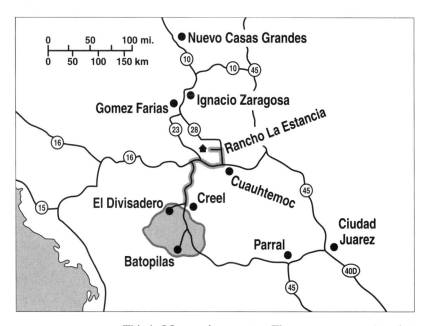

This is **Mennonite** country. The *campos menonitas* that
are on either side of this ride are numbered instead of named,
and each usually consists of 20 or so families. These people
maintain a simple lifestyle. Do not expect to see anything
open in the *campos* on Sunday. The Mennonites believe in no
allegiance, except to God. In the 1920s, they asked the government of Mexico for permission to immigrate, but they
would not accept military service and wanted to establish
their own schools without any swearing of allegiance to the
nation. The government wisely agreed, and the Mennonites
introduced **modern farming techniques** that have benefit-
ted all of Mexico to this day. Their first language is a German
dialect and you will see business signs in German. The region
is known for its *queso menonita* (Mennonite cheese), and a
short visit to a *quesería* is a pleasure. Their white cheddar is
said to be the best made in Mexico.

The last time I was there, the road to the Rancho was five
miles or so of hard-packed dirt. However, if you have any
doubts, stop at the gray house with the stone fence at the turn-
off. This is the home of **Mr. Jacobo Dick,** a local Mennonite
farmer who will let you park your bike in his very safe yard
and drive you down to the Rancho. (You should offer to pay

for this service, but he will probably not accept it.) The Rancho will give you a ride back the next morning.

Connect   Should you wish to connect with the **Colonial Heartland** route at this point, continue straight on Hwy. 16 toward Chihuahua for approximately 110 km (68 mi.) and consult Chapter 6 from that point. ∎

Hotel Rancho la Estancia ($30; tel. 14-16-16-57) has a 4,000-foot paved landing strip that allows the rich and famous to fly into this isolated area to hunt, drink, and relax away from the prying eyes of the world. It was said to have been a favorite of **Bing Crosby** as well as the **"Rat Pack."** Most of its guests today are Europeans who come for the good hunting. It is located in a valley surrounded by small trees, with beautiful, neatly-groomed grounds overflowing with flowers, and it has all the creature comforts, including two swimming pools, two restaurants, a disco, and several bars. Plan to arrive here early in the day so you can enjoy all the amenities at your leisure during the afternoon.

*Ranching in the
remote mountains
is a simple, but
difficult, life.
(Photo by John
Neff)*

5.5 Rancho la Estancia to Deming, NM

Distance   *540 km (335 mi.)*

Features   *Although this is a fairly long day, the roads are good and you will likely be experiencing "border fever." Please remember that you are still in Mexico and resist the temptation to twist the throttle too much. Although you will be traveling mostly through farmland and desert, there is one stretch of curving mountain descent between Babicora and Gomez Farias along this route.*

Turn left (north) onto Hwy. 28 when you rejoin the pavement. After about 140 km (87 mi.), make a right turn in **Babicora** toward Gomez Farias. Continue on to the town of **Buenaventura** where you will hook a left onto Hwy. 10 toward Ignacio Zaragoza. Should you wish to shorten your day and spend another night in Mexico, see the **Nuevo Casas**

A short sit on a bike can make a kid's day.

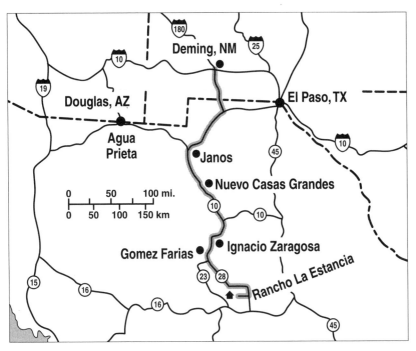

Grandes section on the first day of this chapter. As you approach Nuevo Casas Grandes from the south, the four-lane highway will stop, with the left-turning lane marked CENTRO, and the right lane continuing straight without signage. This road straight ahead will be the city bypass which continues on to Deming. To get to the main drag, turn left and then right on Benito Juarez. The **Motel Hacienda** will be on your left after a few blocks, and you can depart the next morning by continuing directly out of town.

From here, the route will be straightforward, except for an unsigned left turn off Hwy. 2 toward Deming. The turn is 75 km (47 mi.) after you pass **Ascencion,** and it is the only paved road to the left along this stretch. To confirm the turn, note the abandoned customs building you passed at the beginning of this trip.

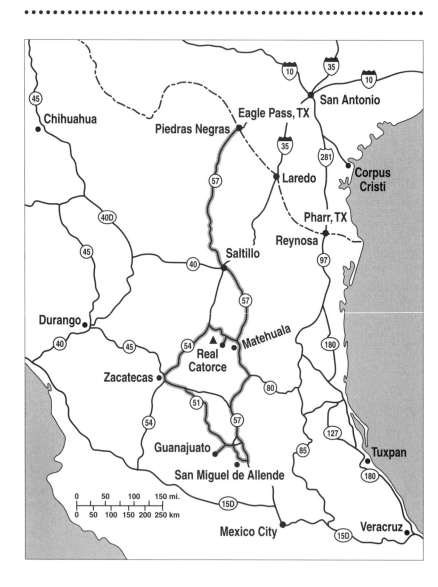

6 The Colonial Heartland

This route is for those who wish to visit the great colonial cities and truly travel through the heart and soul of Mexico's history, from the days of the Spanish occupation to the time of revolution. One city on this route is almost deserted, with a population that once exceeded 40,000 now reduced to less than 700. Other cities have continued to grow and are now major metropolitan areas, yet they still retain the architecture and feel of days of old. In fact, this is one of the most progressive areas in modern Mexico. Note the national monument city of San Miguel de Allende, which is unique in all of Mexico. In addition to its colonial architecture, San Miguel has an eclectic mix of residents ranging from local Indians to international permanent residents, to students at the local language and art schools.

This route is not for those who are looking for twisties and curves. It primarily has long stretches of high desert with beautiful mountains in the distance. The scenery is dramatic, however. While Spanish influence is everywhere, this area is the birthplace of the revolution and it is rich in history. The route is approximately 2,650 km (1,650 mi.) long and consists of seven days of fairly easy riding, but plan on a minimum of ten to twelve days to enjoy what you came to see: the colonial cities. Be careful, many Americans "discover" San Miguel de Allende, smell the roses, and end up spending the rest of their lives there.

6.1 Eagle Pass, Texas, to Saltillo

Distance   *430 km (270 mi.)*

Features   *Today's purpose is to clear the usual border formalities and travel into the interior of Mexico. The route generally consists of good, high-speed highways straight through the desert.*

Eagle Pass, Texas, is a small border city of 21,000 which provides a good overnight stop with all the services you might need prior to entering Mexico. It grew up in the 1850s around **Fort Duncan,** which had been established to protect the area from Indians. Some of the original buildings are still standing. An adequate hotel on Hwy. 57 as you enter the town is the **Holly Inn,** 2421 E. Main Street ($35; tel. 830-773-9261). Secure parking is right outside your room.

Follow Hwy. 57 signs south to reach the border town of **Piedras Negras,** an unusual border crossing in that you get your papers, but you get the papers for your bike 60 km (36 mi.) further south. Also, if you are carrying any contraband, do not plan on getting it through here; they have the most complete inspection of baggage I have ever experienced when entering Mexico. They questioned some aspirin that I had in a plastic bag. To get through Piedras Negras, follow

This remote road through the Mexican desert is a study in solitude.

Mexico, producing automobiles, automobile parts, petro-chemicals, textiles, and tiles. It is also a major transhipment point for the livestock and farm products grown in the area. Thankfully, the industrial complex is situated on the outskirts of town, while the downtown area continues to show its colonial past.

Saltillo was founded in 1577 by the Spanish and soon grew into a major transhipment point on the **Camino Real,** at one time supplying the colonies to the north between Texas and present-day Colorado. It sits in an arid, high mountain valley at more than 5,000 feet, and it is surrounded by the mountains of the **Sierra Madre Oriental.**

The *plaza de armas* is rather barren of local color, but it does contain the **Catedral de Santiago de Saltillo** which is one of the northernmost examples of Spanish church architecture of the late 1700s. You can get a good view of the city from the tower. While the exterior has a magnificent ornate facade, the interior is equally impressive. When lit at night, the *catedral* is truly an impressive sight. The *plaza acuña,* located two blocks north on Calle Allende will give you a much better feel for the town. This shaded square is usually filled in the evenings with families, food vendors, and strolling musicians, and it is surrounded by shops and cafes. The **Mercado Juarez** located on this square is a pleasant place to visit and shop for local handicrafts. If you are a bird lover, the **Museo de las Aves,** located between Allende and Hidalgo just south of the *plaza de armas,* offers wonderful exhibits on nearly 700 species of Mexican birds stuffed and mounted in natural surroundings.

6.2 Saltillo to Real Catorce

Distance   *325 km (195 mi.)*

Features   *Today you will visit the magnificent, nearly-abandoned mining town of Real Catorce. Depending on your circumstances, you could motorcycle the rough road to this wonderful city, or you could stay in Matehuala and hire a ride into town.*

It is only 260 km (160 mi.) of high-speed Hwy. 57 to Matehuala where the nice, clean, and comfortable **Hotel Las Palmas** ($40; tel. 488-2-00-010) will be on your left before you enter the city. The hotel is right out of the 50s, with separate accommodations and secure, carport parking at your room. It also has a very good restaurant. If you are uncomfortable riding 25 km (15 mi.) of rutted cobblestones, the Las Palmas can arrange for a car and driver to take you to Real Catorce; the price will be negotiable, depending on the number of passengers and the amount of time you wish to spend there. **Matehuala** itself, a town of approximately 60,000, is a

On a hot day in the desert highlands, shade will be where you find it.

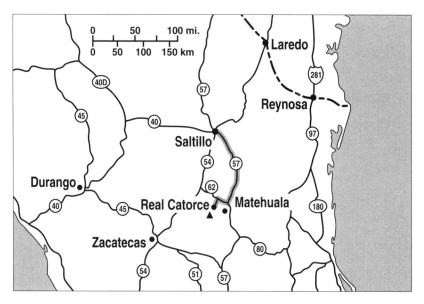

quiet city with few sights to interest the casual visitor. However, an evening sitting around the **Plaza Principal** will gain
you some insight into modern, rural Mexican life.

If you wish to ride to **Real Catorce,** take the well-marked
right turn onto Hwy. 62 about 5 km (3 mi.) before arriving in
Matehuala. The first 30 km (18 mi.) will be a good, two-lane
paved road. As you enter the small town of **Cedral,** just past
the PEMEX, a sign indicates a 90-degree left turn. Continue
straight at this sign to bypass this small town. A private sign
indicating LIBRAMIENTO A REAL DE CATORCE was in existence at this turn the last time I was through there.

At the km 28 milepost, the left turn onto the 25 km (15
mi.) cobblestone road to Real Catorce will be clearly marked.
This road was built in the 1700s to haul out ore, later pro-
cessed silver, and eventually coins from the mint. The
heavily-laden cargo carriers left some deep ruts that still exist
today. If you are riding a dual-sport bike, it is an absolute delight, as it climbs through abandoned mines and villages with
dramatic vistas to the landscape below. In my opinion, it is
passable on a street bike with a rider of reasonable experience, but it will be slow going, especially on a large bike.
Please let your own experience be your guide when deciding
whether or not to travel this road.

As you approach the town, a real adventure awaits: a one-lane tunnel that was originally a mineshaft. The last vehicle going in is given a red stick which he surrenders when he exits, to signal that it is clear to proceed in the other direction. The directors at each end of the tunnel are also in radio contact—but the system is far from perfect! When you get the O.K. to proceed, be alert for people, burros, and maybe even an oncoming bus. If you see headlights, look for a wide place or dig out immediately and get over until the oncoming traffic has passed.

As you exit the tunnel there will be good, flat parking on the left. If you are on a street bike, park here and explore the city on foot. A dual-sport can continue on with no difficulty. You will be greeted by several young men who will offer to guide you through the town and a street full of vendors selling local wares. The **Hotel El Real** ($25; tel. 488-2-25-93) is a wonderful place that is full of ambiance, and it has a good restaurant. Secure parking is available nearby at no extra charge. It is an almost mystic experience to stand on the terrace and watch the sun set over the abandoned housing of the city.

Once a city of over 40,000, Real Catorce now contains only 700 inhabitants. The
abandoned homes create an eerie feeling.

La vida perro—a dog's life in Mexico. (Photo by John Neff)

The origin and founding of **Real Catorce** is unclear. It was officially established in 1779, although records of mining activity in the area date back several years before that. During the 1800s, the rich veins at this 9,000-foot altitude produced vast quantities of silver. So much so, in fact, that a mint was built in the city, and this building still exists, located at the **Jardin Hidalgo.** In the late 1800s, a population in excess of 40,000 enjoyed municipal water, electricity, paved streets, a bullring, and other modern conveniences in this remote location. By 1900, the richer veins had been depleted and a slow decline began. The revolution of 1910 stopped commercial mining activity completely. Today, a few hardy individuals continue to eke out a subsistence by mining the remaining areas.

The local church, **Parroquia de la Purisima Concepcion,** contains the St. Francis shrine. Devotees believe the image in the shrine has the ability to answer prayers and to cleanse believers of sins. Tens of thousands of believers make a pilgrimage to the shrine during the week of October 4th—the only time of the year you won't find the city almost deserted. The area around Real Catorce is also sacred to the **Huicholes,** who give special significance to the hallucinogenic cactus known as *peyote,* which grows in this area. They visit this area in the spring to collect the *peyote* and perform various religious rituals. Because of these pilgrimages, many believe Real Catorce to be one of the "power points" on earth. It certainly has an atmosphere all to itself.

6.3 Real Catorce to Zacatecas

Distance   *300 km (190 mi.)*

Features   *This is a straightforward day of good, high desert riding with an encounter with a modern, yet still colonial, Mexican city.*

If you have spent the night in Real Catorce, retrace your route and turn left at the intersection with Hwy. 62. If you stayed in Matehuala, follow the directions to Real Catorce without the left turn onto the cobblestone. Continue on Hwy. 62 until the intersection with Hwy. 54 at marker 112 km (66 mi.) in **San Tiburico,** where you will take a left turn south toward Zacatecas. There will be snack shops and restaurants at this intersection. Try **La Cabana.**

From here it will be a straight shot down Hwy. 54 to Zacatecas—and I mean straight! For some reason I always get lost entering the city itself, however. The dramatic elevation changes prevented the streets of the city from being laid out on a grid, and it gets confusing, with various one-way streets heading away from where you wish to go. Enjoy the

Open spaces and large cattle ranches consume vast areas of the central grasslands.

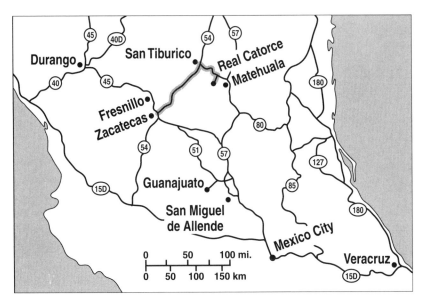

wonderful colonial architecture as you wander through them. Follow the main four-lane boulevard to the *plaza de armas.* When you are truly lost, use the "taxi trick" I describe in Chapter 1. The **Hotel Posada Tolosa,** Juan de Tolosa #811 ($30; tel. 492-2-51-05), located only one block off the *plaza de armas* will provide comfortable, basic accommodations, with a parking garage for your bike. It can be noisy, however, so earplugs can be helpful.

Zacatecas, a city of approximately 350,000 people, rests in a narrow, high valley (8,200 feet). Steep sides lead up to the peaks which overlook the activity below. The sharply slanting terrain has created a maze of one-way streets, switchbacks, and dead ends which are best explored on foot with a local guide. Zacatecas was a mining center even before the Spanish arrived in the New World, but the discovery of a very rich vein in 1546 set the stage for the establishment of one of the richest mining towns in the world. Mining remains a major factor in the economy even today. Zacatecas is also the site of one of the major battles in the **Mexican Revolution,** a fact noted by various statues, museums, and exhibits.

The tallest peak, **Cerro de la Bufa,** is served by a cable car and road. I would suggest you take a taxi to the top to see the huge **equestrian statues** of three leaders of the Mexican Revolution. Francisco "Pancho" Villa, Felipe Angeles, and Panfilo Natera stand in all their glory, celebrating their 1914 victory over the opposing Huerta forces. There is a **small museum** containing uniforms, newspaper clippings, photos, weapons, and other artifacts of the battle. From here you can take a 10-minute ride over the city on the **cable car** *(teleférico)*, which offers spectacular views. Near the cable car station, the early silver mine **El Eden** is open for tours. You will see the rickety ladders and ropes the Indian slaves used to haul ore up seven stories of sheer cliff. They worked until they were killed or died. In an ironic twist, there is now a disco at the bottom of the mine that is open in the evening for your enjoyment.

From the mine exit, it is a short, enjoyable walk back to the *plaza de armas*. In this area of the city, there are many buildings, sights, and museums of interest. I suggest you find a local, English-speaking guide to show them to you. Make sure to see the **Catedral de Zacatecas,** which has been called "the ultimate expression of Mexican baroque." The highlight of this church is its impressive main facade which faces Hi-

At a rest stop in the Mennonite farmland between Chihuahua and Creel, riders pause to smell the delicious air and observe cowboys tending their farm. (Photo by Dan Kennedy)

dalgo. In building this magnificent edifice, the silver barons spared no expense. The interior is plain and somewhat disappointing after viewing the facade.

The **Teatro Calderion,** built in 1832 and renovated in 1891, is located on Hidalgo just down from the *plaza de armas* and is a wonderful example of late 19th-century theaters. It remains in use today. A stroll through will put you in another era and social setting. The **Palacio de Gobierno,** located on the *plaza de armas,* presents an interesting, if not very colonial facade. The **Mercado Gonzalez Ortega** located on the south side of the *catedral* was, at one time, the main market of the city. It is a wonderful building right out of the past with large wrought-iron columns forming *portales.* Today, the main floor has been converted into trendy boutiques and there are cafes serving regional specialties on the bottom.

Zacatecas is not on the usual tourist path and the number of foreign visitors each year remains small. However, it is a wonderful Spanish colonial city which is still thriving today. Plan on spending at least one full day there.

6.4 Zacatecas to San Miguel de Allende

Distance   *320 km (200 mi.)*

Features   *This will be an easy day of high desert riding. Expect generally good roads with light traffic. At the end of the day you will be in one of Mexico's most famous national monument cities.*

Getting out of Zacatecas without getting lost should be easy—but it is impossible for me. I usually hire a taxi to guide me out of the city. From the *plaza de armas,* go straight on Ave. Hidalgo (one-way) and watch for the signs for Hwy. 115 toward Fresnillo. You will find yourself on a large circle above the city with several places to pull over and admire the view or take pictures. After several miles, follow signs at the round-about for Hwy. 45 toward Mexico City/Guadalupe.

Now how will I get this home? Ceramics are a specialty of Dolores Hidalgo.

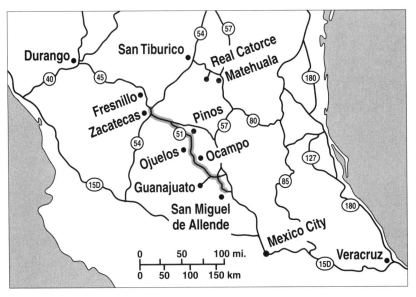

Just past **Guadalupe,** pick up signs for Hwy. 51 toward San Luis Potosi. Twelve miles after this intersection, turn right on Hwy. 166 toward Pinos (your map may indicate this as Hwy. 51). This is good road with magnificent desert scenery. The wonderful **mission church** in the small village of **Villa Gonzales Ortega** is worth the short, two-block trip off the main road.

After 70 km (42 mi.), in the small town of **Pinos,** follow the signs toward Ojuelos; the highway will now be definitely marked as 51. From there, follow the signs to Ocampo. About 155 km (96 mi.) after Pinos you will be approaching Dolores Hidalgo, a small town worth a stop (see sidebar). Just outside town, there will be a PEMEX on the left; less than a half mile later there will be another PEMEX on the left at an intersection landscaped with ceramic jugs. Turn left at this station. There will be no sign.

Continue straight down a street crowded with ceramic shops to a T-intersection, turn left toward San Luis de la Paz, and pick up signs for San Miguel de Allende. The road becomes more hilly and curvy over the next 35 km (21 mi.) to San Miguel. Continue straight into town and you will soon reach the center square, **El Jardin.**

The delightful **Hotel Posada de San Francisco** ($35; tel. 415-2-72-13) is located on the square in the center of the action. It is next to the police station and provides secure parking several blocks away. After you've unloaded your bike, you can ride over to the parking. The cab ride back will be about $1.

The national monument town of **Dolores Hidalgo** is known as the "Cradle of National Independence." At midnight on September 15, 1810, **Father Miguel Hidalgo y Costilla** called his parishioners to the local church by ringing the bell. He then made the adored **Grito de Dolores** speech declaring Mexican independence. Today, the 16th of Sep-

Father Miguel Hidalgo y Costilla

Popularly known as the "Father of Mexican Independence," Father Miguel Hidalgo y Costilla was quite an unusual person. Born in 1753, he attended college and was ordained as a priest. Although he later taught college and became a rector, some of his views and ways led to a visit with the Inquisition in 1800. It is said that he questioned some of the basic beliefs of the Catholic Church, such as the virgin birth and the infallibility of the pope. It is also said that he gambled and had a mistress. Hidalgo escaped the Inquisition but was sent to the small town of Dolores in 1804 to be the local priest.

Hidalgo became involved with the move for independence when he met Ignacio Allende, and in 1810 he issued his now famous call for independence, the Grito de Dolores. At this point he became a true revolutionary and led troops as they attempted to free Mexico from Spanish dominance. As a result of this and his continuing public speeches against the church, he was excommunicated on October 13, 1810. As the Spanish gradually gained ground against the Mexicans, Miguel Hidalgo was captured and shot by a firing squad on July 30, 1811.

In a final, bizarre twist in this man's history, Hidalgo's head, along with three others, Allende's included, were returned to Guanajuato and hung from a public building near the main square, where they remained for almost ten years. This backfired on the Spanish in that rather than intimidate the Mexicans, it became a battle cry. The hooks that held the heads are still on the building today.   ∎

Churches are around every corner in San Miguel de Allende.

tember is still celebrated as **Independence Day** and politicians throughout Mexico repeat an altered version of the *grito.* The old church bell is rung only on this day each year. The home of Father Hidalgo, at Morelos #1, is now a **museum** containing items relating to his life and times, and there is also a statue of Hidalgo on the main square.

Dolores Hidalgo is a pleasant town with a wonderful central plaza. It is noted for its hand-glazed ceramics and the streets are lined with various stores selling colorful jugs, plates, tiles, and anything else that can be conceived in ceramic. Factor in an hour or two to explore this town.

San Miguel de Allende, pop. 80,000, is the crown jewel of Mexican national monument cities and a favorite of Americans, many of whom retire here. Even more have homes

An uneducated Indian, inspired by a picture on a postcard, oversaw the building of the facade of this church in San Miguel de Allende (Courtesy of Pancho Villa Moto-Tours)

they use for only part of the year. San Miguel has several arts and crafts schools that attract **international students** of all persuasions. It is also known for its Spanish language schools and many people come to stay a month and learn the language, although the multicultural flavor of San Miguel does not make Spanish necessary; of the many languages spoken here, very little will be Spanish. The protected colonial architecture, monuments, fountains, and churches, as well as the eclectic mix of people make San Miguel de Allende a delight.

San Miguel was founded in 1542 by a Franciscan friar, **Fray Juan de San Miguel,** as an outpost to bring the Christian religion to the "pagan" Indians. By 1555, the road connecting it with Mexico City had been completed and a fort was established to protect silver shipments. During the early 1800s, this city was the home of **Ignacio Allende** during the Mexican Revolution. Although Allende was captured and

To teenagers the world over, giggles abound. These pretty girls are delighted that we want their picture.

Children will add much to your Mexican experience. These two are prepared to drive a hard bargain.

killed by the Spanish in 1811, the revolution was successful ten years later. In 1826 the town was renamed in his honor. It was designated a national monument city in 1926.

Life in San Miguel revolves around the central square, **El Jardin,** a most pleasant place to spend an hour of two in the evening. San Miguel's biggest attraction is the parish church, **La Parroquia.** Its many steeples will remind you of the Gothic churches one sees in Europe—and that is not merely a coincidence. In the late 19th century, after two hundred years in existence, the facade of the structure was rebuilt by **Zeferino Gutierrez,** a local Indian with no formal education. His only "plans" were picture postcards of European

You can enjoy the view of a colonial church while relaxing on the porch of your hotel.

Shiny shoes are very important to Mexican men. It will cost you about a dollar to have
your motorcycle boots shined.

churches. Since his postcards showed only the fronts of the churches, the rear of this one maintains a style more typical of Mexico.

A visit to the **Museo Historico de San Miguel de Allende,** Calle Cunda de Allende 1, has a fine overview of the history of this city and the surrounding area, as well as exhibits on Ignacio Allende and the struggle for independence.

The *biblioteca pública* serves as a kind of clearing house for the expatriate community and provides copies of the local English language newspaper. A notice board lists activities that might interest a visitor, apartments for rent, and other things. Take a few minutes to read these notices and you will get an appreciation of what it would be like to live in this fine city as an American. You could also arrange a tour of some of the town's finer homes and gardens here. San Miguel has many other pleasant plazas and a dazzling array of other churches to visit. Turn almost any corner and you will be in for another pleasant surprise. If you are interested in art, there are several galleries. Shopping for art, handicrafts, and jewelry can be a major activity for many visitors to San Miguel.

6.5 San Miguel to Guanajuato

· ·

Distance   *200 km, round trip from San Miguel (125 mi.)*

Features   *A day trip to the colonial city of Guanajuato offers many sights worth a visit and quite a bit of history, too. After you leave Dolores Hidalgo, the road will climb and twist until you have delightful views of the broad plain below. You will encounter quite an altitude change, so don't judge your gear requirements based on the temperature in San Miguel. As you approach Guanajuato, there will be fantastic views of the town below you.*

From El Jardin, head south on the one-way street going downhill (Cuna de Allende) and you will soon come to a T-intersection where the signs to Dolores Hidalgo are clearly marked to the left. Follow these signs out of the city. After 40 km (24 mi.), begin to follow the signs toward Guanajuato. A four-lane divided street will bypass most of the town. If you did not stop to visit here on the way down and wish to now, just follow the *centro* signs. From this point, get prepared for 60 km (36 mi.) of great motorcycling.

As you approach the city, one of the most famous churches in Mexico, officially known as **La Iglesia de San Cayetano,** but commonly called **La Valenciana,** will be on your left about halfway down the hill; it is well worth a visit.

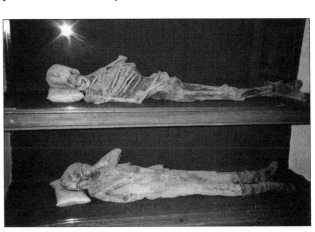

Prepare yourself for a gruesome but fascinating experience at the Museum of Mummies in Guanajuato. (Photo by John Neff)

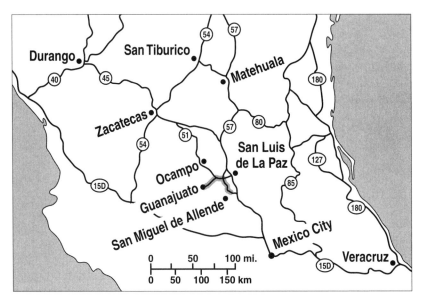

A view of the Valenciana mine is available from the parking lot on the right side of the road next to the church. This is the most prolific of Mexican silver mines, at one time producing almost 25 percent of the world's silver; it's still in operation today. When the daughter of the mine's owner got married in the nearby church, he had the path from his house lain with silver ingots.

Guanajuato is a large metropolitan city that can have serious traffic problems. I suggest you park your bike at a hotel with secure parking and explore the city on foot. By following the signs toward Leon or Silao, you will find the hotel **Hacienda de las Cobos** on your left, at Padre Hidalgo #3 and Ave. Juarez #153 ($45; tel. 473-203-50). It has secure parking in a courtyard and a back door off the patio so you can walk to the sights in and around the central plaza. Should you wish to stay overnight in Guanajuato (which I highly recommend), this is a more than adequate hotel. After a delightful visit to this town, retrace your route to San Miguel.

If you don't wish to return to San Miguel, just retrace your route through Dolores Hidalgo toward San Miguel. Shortly after clearing the city, a clearly-marked left turn onto Hwy. 110 toward San Luis de la Paz will intersect with Hwy. 57 toward San Luis Potosi after 35 km (22 mi.). This will save you

Guanajuato, a city of churches, rests in a deep valley. (Courtesy of Pancho Villa Moto-Tours)

approximately 70 km (45 mi.) and more than an hour. From this point, pick up the route for Day 6 from this intersection.

With a population of approximately 120,000, **Guanajuato** was once the home of some of the richest people in the world. Since the city sits in a high valley surrounded by mountains, the streets are not laid out in a grid pattern and it can be quite confusing to navigate. It is best explored by foot. Many of the streets run underground, built inside old mineshafts and river courses. You can hire a taxi to take you on a short tour.

The vast lodes of silver and gold located near Guanajuato led to the building of some magnificent mansions which are still in existence today. At one time almost a third of the world's silver was mined in the area. Guanajuato also played a crucial role in the **Mexican War of Independence,** and there are many good museums documenting this period. Today, Guanajuato is a vibrant, bustling city with a university whose more than 15,000 students add a spirit of youth to this historic colonial city. The city is also known for music: bands play, strolling groups fill the plazas, and young men, called *estudiantinas,* wander the streets until all hours of the night playing to all who are willing to listen (and a few who are not).

With the discovery of the **La Valenciana mine** in 1558, the city rapidly grew in population and wealth. At the start of the War of Independence, it was one of the most prosperous cities in all of New Spain. Although it was the third city to be captured by the rebels in 1810, it was the first of any size. It was quickly retaken by the Spanish, however, who punished the population by holding a "lottery of death" where the winners were killed.

Because there are many sights to see in Guanajuato, plan for an overnight stay, if at all possible. The **Alhondiga de Granaditas,** originally a granary and later a jail and fortress, now contains an excellent museum. When the rebels first attempted to take Guanajuato, the Spanish and their supporters fled to this building and locked themselves in. On September 28, 1810, a young rebel named **Jose de los Reyes Martinez** managed to set the gates ablaze before being killed by gunfire, thus allowing the rebels to enter and overcome the Spanish. This young Indian, known as **El Pipila,** became a national hero and a statue of him with his torch sits on top of a hill in the center of the city. For ten years after the Spanish retook Guanajuato, the **severed heads** of Hidalgo, Allende, Jimenez, and Aldama hung in metal cages from the corners of the roof of this building. The hooks are still here. The building now houses an excellent history museum as well as an art gallery. Colorful and graphic murals by **Chavez Morado** line the stairwells.

The **Jardin de la Union** is the center of the action in Guanajuato. In the evenings, nearby university students gather on the tree-shaded grounds to watch the ever-changing social scene. The **Teatro Juarez,** built from 1873 to 1903, is located on the Jardin de la Union. The interior decor is definitely French and it reflects the wealth of the people of Guanajuato during its construction. Not for the faint of heart or the weak of stomach, the very unusual **Museo de las Momias** (Mummy Museum) contains the remains of bodies that were preserved after burial by the climate and soil conditions. It contains over a hundred mummies of all types, including babies and pregnant women. Located at Calz. del Panteon, the museum is best visited by taxi.

6.6 San Miguel to Saltillo

Distance   *600 km (370 mi.)*

Features   *The departure route from San Miguel will give you a spectacular overview of the city. Afterwards, you will again encounter the altiplano (high desert). Expect a rather long day on high-speed, four-lane road with a few curves that twist over a pass or two.*

From El Jardin, head south on Cuna de Allende, and after two blocks turn right at your first opportunity. At the T-intersection, turn left and follow the cobblestone street as it winds its way up the hill. If you get turned around, just ask for directions to the PEMEX. Soon you will see a wonderful over-look with ample parking. After a stop for a mandatory pic-

This handsome lad is waiting for a ride back to the country. (Photo by Dwight Carlos Hughes)

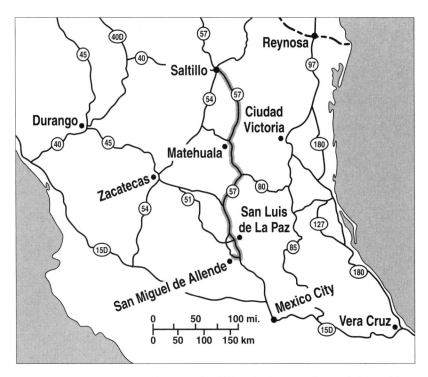

ture, continue up the hill to the PEMEX. Go straight, and in a
very short time the turn to San Luis Potosi will be clearly
marked on your left (Hwy. 111).

Proceed 35 km (21 mi.) to the intersection with Hwy. 57.
You will need to take the overpass over the large four-lane
road and U-turn to get on the highway. From this point, follow the signs toward San Luis Potosi. As you approach the
city, take the road to the Monterrey *cuota,* a 25-peso ($2.50)
toll road which bypasses the city itself. To choose Monterrey
libre instead, follow Hwy. 57 toward Monterrey.

Connect   Approximately 70 km (42 mi.) up Hwy. 57, a sign will indicate an intersection with Hwy. 80 toward Ciudad del Maiz. If
you wish to connect to the **Veracruz** route, turn right here.
The first 130 km (78 mi.) continues through high desert terrain. As you leave **Ciudad del Maiz,** the moist air will hit
you almost immediately, the lush vegetation of palm trees,
ferns, and tropical plants replacing the dry desert cactus and
yuccas. It is an amazing transformation in a remarkably small
distance. This is one of the best motorcycle roads I have ever

Views like this one along the high desert make it hard to concentrate on the road.

Motorcycling just doesn't get any better than this.

A stop at a Mexican "convenience store" makes for a nice break.

ridden in Mexico, as it descends, twists, and turns through the jungle.

At the intersection with Hwy. 85, turn south for 70 km (42 mi.) heading toward Ciudad Valles. The **Hotel Valles** will be on this main highway as you enter town (see Chapter 7 for details). I cannot stress enough how delighted you will be by both the drive and the dramatic change in climate. Highly recommended! ■

If you are proceeding on Hwy. 57, it is another 330 km (200 mi.) of high-speed road to **Saltillo** and the **Hotel Fuente** (see Day 1).

6.7 Saltillo to Eagle Pass, Texas

Distance   430 km (270 mi.)

Features   The purpose of this day is to arrive back in the U.S. safe and sound. Just follow Hwy. 57 for some high-speed driving to the border. To reach the border just reverse the routing for Day 1.

Today you will retrace your route from Day 1 along Hwy. 57. Remember to turn in your motorcycle permits prior to exiting

A ready smile is your reward whenever you travel in Mexico. (Courtesy of Pancho Villa Moto-Tours)

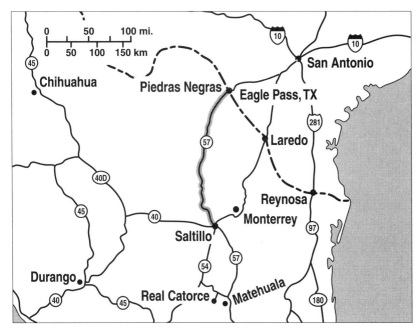

Mexico. You will probably be experiencing some "border fever," but don't let the good road conditions lull you into a false sense of security—this is still a day's ride in Mexico.

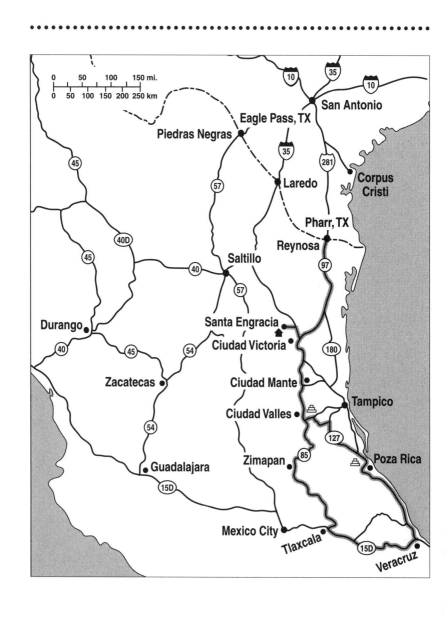

7 Jungles, Veracruz, and Indian Villages

●●

If you like remote areas, colorful *zócolos,* twisties, jungle, and cultures that have not changed over time, this is the route for you. This trip consists of approximately 2,300 km (1,430 mi.) and eight days of riding, some of which is the best in all of Mexico. You will encounter some very old Indian cultures, as well as the vibrant city of Veracruz. To truly enjoy this route, plan on ten to twelve days minimum .

7.1 Pharr, Texas, to Ciudad Mante

Distance *330 km (205 mi.)*

Features *This day is set up to get you through the border formalities and into the interior of Mexico on mostly high-speed, two-lane road through savannah and scrub. Consider taking a side trip to the fishing lodge on Lake Guerrero before you ride through the Cañon de la Galena south of Ciudad Victoria.*

There is a plentiful supply of national chain hotels in **Pharr, Texas,** all of which are located on the main drag through town. Upon leaving your hotel, continue south toward Reynosa. As you approach the border, there will be several 24-hour, drive-through *cambios* where you can quickly and easily change dollars to pesos. After crossing the border

Mountainous back roads with unbelievable scenery will have you stopping often.

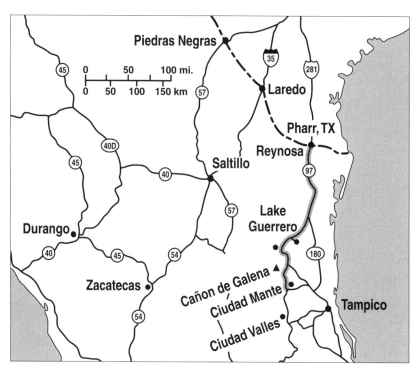

bridge, stop at the clearly-marked immigration facilities to get papers for yourself. When you explain that you will also need a vehicle permit, they will provide you with a map to the facility a few blocks away, off the main route. On your way there, pay attention to the right turn to Matamoros, as you must retrace your way to this intersection after your paperwork has been completed.

Reynosa, a modern industrial city of approximately 370,000, is a typical border town and not to my liking. It has the usual facilities for casual day or night visitors to Mexico, but little flavor and almost nothing in the way of historical interest. As with all border towns, I recommend you just continue on into the interior.

Ten km. (6 mi.) after the left turn toward Matamoros, you'll see the right turn to Hwy. 97 toward Ciudad Victoria. Approximately 28 km (17 mi.) after leaving the vehicle permit facility you will reach the customs and document checkpoint. (This will be a straightforward, boring drive.) After 113 km (70 mi.) on Hwy. 97, take the obvious right turn onto

Hwy. 101 toward Ciudad Victoria. After approximately 140 km (85 mi.), you will be approaching the city.

Side Trip   **Lake Guerrero** is world famous for its **bass fishing** and sportsmen from all over fly in to try their luck—although, I have been told that "luck" is not necessary here. If you want to see how upper-class fishermen "rough it" at the lake, I recommend a short side trip to **Hacienda Lago Guerrero.** This excursion will also give you a chance to actually get into the desert that has been flashing by all day. As you are driving toward Ciudad Victoria, watch for the large sign on the left that indicates the camp. After just a few short miles on the pavement, another large sign will indicate a left turn down a dirt road. This 5 km (3 mi.) road to the *hacienda* is well-maintained and can be easily traversed on a street bike. The road ends at the hacienda, which can make for a great lunch stop if the time is right. The owner, Steve Murray, is from College Station, Texas, and he is a most gracious host. For more information on this top-flight facility, call them at 800-567-8824. ■

As you approach Ciudad Victoria, watch for the left turn to Hwy. 85 toward Tampico, which will allow you to bypass the city itself. From here, follow Hwy. 85 signs toward Ciudad Mante or Ciudad Valles.

   Ciudad Victoria, a city of approximately 250,000, is a clean, pleasant, and fairly modern city, but it does not offer much in the way of attractions. Because the area lacked ores

Siestas are a great Mexican tradition. (Photo by John Neff)

Some motels offer very secure parking.

suitable for mining, it was mostly ignored by the Spanish. Founded in 1750, Ciudad Victoria (named for Mexico's first president) became the state capital in 1825. It was occupied by U.S. troops during the **Mexican-American War** and was prominent during the revolution of 1910–20. Today, as a transportation hub at the intersection of several major highways, it offers all the goods and services one would need.

On leaving Ciudad Victoria behind, the scenery will become more interesting as Hwy. 85 twists and turns through the **Cañon de la Galena.** You should arrive in Ciudad Mante 70 km (43 mi.) after leaving Ciudad Victoria.

Ciudad Mante (population 120,000) is a rather nondescript Mexican farming center for processing the sugar cane grown in the surrounding fields. It has no first-class hotel accommodations, as it is not a regular overnight stop. However, it can be a good, attainable destination for your first night in Mexico, especially if you took the side trip to the lake or were delayed at the border. The best place to stay is the **Hotel Monterrey,** located on the highway in the center of town at Calle Juarez 503 N ($30; tel. 123-2-27-12). The accommodations will be basic, but it is clean and has *agua caliente,* secure parking, and a restaurant. Should you have stamina and daylight to spare, the **Hotel Valles** 100 km (62 mi.) down the road is a much better facility (see Day 7).

7.2 Ciudad Mante to Poza Rica

Distance   *350 km (220 mi.)*

Features   *Your goal today will be to reach Poza Rica, visit the El Tajin ruins, and see the Voladores perform their "flying act." It is easy to get lost, as portions of the roads on this route are in pretty poor condition and are often covered with sugar cane debris—so don't let the distance fool you. I suggest an early start as there will be much to see.*

Continue south on Hwy. 85 toward **Ciudad Valles.** You will reach Valles after 100 km (62 mi.) of fairly straightforward riding through vast savannah.

The Voladores at Poza Rica reenact an ancient Indian religious tradition for the tourists.

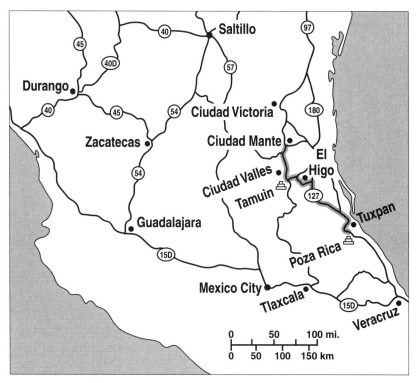

Connect Should you wish to connect with the **Colonial Heartland** trip at this point, there is an amazing road approximately 30 km (19 mi.) south of Ciudad Mante. A right turn onto Hwy. 80 toward Ciudad del Maiz will take you up a twisting, turning jungle highway; in only 90 km (56 mi.) you will go from tropical rain forests to arid desert. Continue through **Ciudad del Maiz** on Hwy. 80. After 130 km (80 mi.) of high desert, you will intersect with Hwy. 57 and pick up that route from there. I cannot stress enough how delightful and dramatic this drive will be. ∎

Ciudad Valles, a city of over 300,000, has long been a stopover for motorists traveling the **Pan-American Highway.** With the completion of a modern, high desert highway to Mexico City, the tourist business fell off dramatically, however. Valles itself is a commercial center which processes and transports the coffee, sugar, and oranges grown on nearby farms and plantations. The **Hotel Valles** is a wonderful place to spend the night (see Day 7) and from there you could do the side trip I suggest to Ciudad del Maiz.

Just as you pass through Ciudad Valles, you'll see a clearly-marked left turn onto Hwy. 70 toward Tampico. After 30 km (19 mi.) of pleasant two-lane road, take the right turn onto Hwy. 120 toward El Higo. From this point, you will have a 70 km (44 mi.) ride through rural Mexico. The Huastec Indian ruins, called either **El Consuelo** or **Ruinas Tamuin,** are just a short distance down the road. The site is quite famous and you can access it easily from this route, however, the ruins at El Tajin are much more extensive and restored. This civilization peaked between 800 and 1200 C.E. The **Huastec** still exist today and you will see many as you travel the remainder of this route.

From Tamuin to El Higo it is only 40 km (25 mi.) to the left turn toward Tampico/Panuco. If you reach the actual city, you will have gone too far. This road was well-worn the last time I was through. Another 30 km (19 mi.) later, you will be at a T-intersection with Hwy. 105. Turn right toward Tuxpan. Expect this road to be in very poor condition with pot holes and deteriorating pavement. Continue for approximately 30 km (19 mi.) to the left turn onto Hwy. 127, still toward

These women are selling their hand-made wares.

El Tajin and The Voladores

El Tajin is the most extensively uncovered and restored Huastec site in Mexico. Although you can now visit a huge area, hundreds more pyramids and buildings are still covered by the thick jungle growth. Scholars believe the city peaked between 600 and 1200 C.E. and was an important religious center. It contains palaces, ball courts, houses, and temples. Its biggest attraction is the Pyramid of the Niches, which is seven stories tall and covered with carved sandstone panels depicting various rulers, as well as the god Quetzalcoatl.

The ball courts were used to play a game similar to soccer. The object of the game was to get a small, rubber-like ball through a hoop well above the players' heads. Sometimes the game was played for life or death, but it is uncertain whether the winner or loser was sacrificed to the gods.

At the modern entranceway you can see the performance of the Voladores rite several times a day, although it does not appear to follow a set schedule. Some believe the performance was originally a fertility rite, but others disagree. Five men in Indian attire climb a very tall pole topped by a platform. One sits on top, plays a flute and beats a drum. The other four attach themselves to ropes that reach to the ground. At the end of the flute and drum session, they launch themselves into the air and slowly twirl around the pole until they reach the ground. Whatever the original reason for this, the flyers now earn their living from tourist donations. ■

Tuxpan. Approximately 190 km (118 mi.) from the turn onto Hwy. 105, and 40 km (25 mi.) before reaching the city, you will need to turn right onto Hwy. 180 toward Castillo/Poza Rica to stay out of the city of Tuxpan.

From this point, continue to follow signs for Poza Rica. The right turn to the ruins of **El Tajin** will be clearly marked as you pass through the city. This 40 km (25 mi.) round trip is a worthy diversion (see sidebar). Some spend days exploring the vast grounds. After your visit, return to Hwy. 180 and

The Huastecs

The Huastecs civilization can be dated back to approximately 1000 B.C.E. and reached its height between 800 and 1300 C.E. It occupied an area from the central gulf coast of Mexico to the jungles on the eastern slopes of the Sierra Madre Oriental. These peace-loving people had a distinct language and were primarily farmers. They produced beautiful stone carvings, pottery, and jewelry made from shells and feathers. As avid enemies of the Aztecs, the Huastecs quickly formed an alliance with the Spanish, providing more than ten thousand warriors to help conquer this great nation. Following that, disease, slavery, and harsh treatment under the Spanish quickly brought on the demise of their culture and civilization, as it did to so many other tribes of the time. Today, approximately 100,000 of these people still exist in small villages, living in thatched roof huts in an area north and west of Veracruz. You see them most often in small villages in the Tamazunchale area wearing their colorfully embroidered *quechquémitls* depicting animals, flowers, and trees of life.

The Huastec originated the legend of the god Quetzalcoatl, a benevolent god who had sailed away to the east because of an indiscretion, specifically to return in 1519 to reclaim his rightful throne. Because Quetzalcoatl was said to be fair-skinned and bearded, Cortes fit this picture well and played it to the hilt. The Aztecs delayed acting against the Spaniards for fear that Quetzalcoatl had returned to rule, and this gave the Spanish an important advantage.

The Mexican government has spent most of its efforts studying and renovating the ruins of the Maya and Aztec nations, rather than those of the Huastec culture. The best example of a Huastec city is Tamuin, located approximately 30 km (19 mi.) east of Ciudad Valles on Hwy. 110. ∎

*Modern ways are slow to invade small Mexican villages. (Photo by
Dwight Carlos Hughes)*

continue south. As you are leaving the city, the very upscale,
modern **Poza Rica Inn,** Blvd. Poza Rica km 4.5 ($55; tel.
782-3-1922), will be on a hill to your left. It has secure parking and the rooms and amenities are very good.

7.3 Poza Rica to Veracruz

Distance   *260 km (161 mi.)*

Features   *This is a straightforward day of riding through the lowlands of the state of Veracruz to the wonderful and historic city of Veracruz itself. A short side trip to the last home of Hernan Cortes will give you a chance to visit a sleepy Mexican village. There are also opportunities to visit some ancient Huastec sites along the route.*

From the Poza Rica Inn, take a left to continue south. After 15 km (9 mi.), the left turn onto Hwy. 180 toward Veracruz will be clearly marked. All you need to remember for the remainder of this day is to watch for the signs for Hwy. 180 toward Veracruz.

Side Trip   **Jalapa,** a city of approximately 400,000, is the capital of the state of Veracruz and a center for learning. If you wish to get

Open-air markets offer a wonderful way to purchase fresh fruit to carry on the road.
(Photo by Dwight Carlos Hughes)

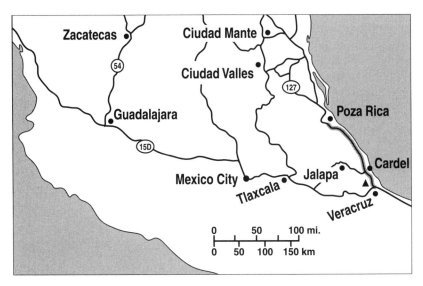

a real feel for the history of this area, as well as the Huastec, Olmec, and Toltec cultures, this should be a "must" stop. The **Museo de Antropologia de la Universidad Veracruzana,** an open-air facility surrounded by botanical gardens, contains many artifacts from these cultures including seven massive Olmec stone head carvings. Although most people are attracted to Jalapa to visit the museum, the town itself is worth some time, as the university students add much to the beautiful flower-covered plazas and lush areas of tropical vegetation. You should consider an overnight stay. Approximately 35 km (23 mi.) before Veracruz at the town of **Cardel,** the right turn toward Jalapa will be clearly marked. Round trip, it is approximately 140 km (84 mi.) from Hwy. 180. ■

Side Trip   Approximately 215 km (134 mi.) from Ciudad Valles, a right turn toward **La Antiga** can provide a very short diversion and an interesting visit to a historical site. In this tiny Mexican village, the central square is where **Hernan Cortes** headquartered for a time before he moved to Veracruz. Right on the square, the **ruins of his last home** are marked by a small, rusting sign. There have been no attempts to restore or preserve it, which pretty much reflects feelings of the Mexican people toward this great *conquistador.* This is a delightful small village and a walk around the square, and a visit to the

ruins and church is well worth the trip. This church, the first
one built in Mexico, baptized the first Indian. ■

After your visit, return the short distance to Hwy. 180 and
continue south. The signage to the *zócolo* in Veracruz is not
very clear. Just follow signs to the centro or zócolo until you
cross over a large viaduct. About a block later, a large zócolo
sign will indicate a left turn. Take this left and pay no attention to signs after this. The next right, and then again the next
right, will have you in the zócolo in four blocks. After coming off the viaduct, you will be very near your destination. If
in doubt, ask a taxi to guide you.

Have trombone,
will play—for
only a few pesos.
(Courtesy of
Mexico's Ministry
of Tourism)

The friendliness you will find everywhere in Mexico should be returned at every opportunity.

The **Hotel Imperial** ($40; tel. 29-32-30-31), in the middle of one of the sides of the square, is a very pleasant place to stay. It has a fantastic elevator, the rooms are large, and the bathrooms more than adequate. The ambiance and location are unbeatable. They will direct you to secure parking nearby. Because the *zócolo* will be right outside your room, earplugs may come in handy.

Veracruz (meaning "true cross") is a delight to visit. This vibrant, busy port town of over one million people has a feel like no other in Mexico, the direct result of a rich history and the mixture of many cultures. The almost frantic nightlife is centered around the *zócolo,* with strolling bands, gaiety, clowns, hawkers, and even slack-rope walkers. The citizens of Veracruz, known as *jarachos,* are a fun-loving and laid-back group.

The *zócalo* in Veracruz is one of the liveliest in all of Mexico, reflecting the city's fun-loving population. On any given night, the plaza will be filled with lovers, families, children, hookers, vendors, and beggars—all being serenaded by wandering mariachis, guitarists, and other people trying to outdo the rest to get your attention. On some evenings, a formal band will try to overcome this crescendo, but it is usually to no avail. Have a nice dinner in one of the sidewalk cafes and you'll enjoy a front row seat to all the commotion.

Shortly after the Spanish landed in 1519, Veracruz became a major port. During the colonial era, millions of dollars worth of gold and silver were shipped through here on the way to Spain, as it was the only "official" port of entry into and out of Mexico until 1870. If you take the time to read this port's long, detailed history, you will learn of **numerous invasions,** the most dramatic of which occurred in 1683, when the French pirate **Laurent de Gaff** and his men held the city and its population captive while they robbed, raped, and rampaged before departing with their loot. It was the port of Veracruz that **General Winfield Scott** and the U.S. Army forces chose as a beachhead for the march on Mexico City in 1847. **Napoleon III** also sent his conquering forces through here in 1861. In addition, African slaves were used to load and unload the cargos of the ships, and many Cubans also entered and worked here, making Veracruz an international melting pot. New rulers arrived here and old ones departed or fled through here. Leaders of various revolutionary groups were jailed here. After treatments for malaria and yellow fever were developed, Veracruz became the major port city it is today.

The best way to see Veracruz is to park your bike and hire a guide to show you around. Some things not to miss:

- The **Paseo del Malecon,** the street that runs along the waterfront, offers excellent places to sit and observe the activities of the harbor: the loading and unloading of freighter cargos, the never-ending chores of the fishing fleet, and, usually, the maneuvering of Mexican naval vessels. There are several open-air restaurants along the thruway where you can sit and enjoy a meal or drink and watch until your heart is content.

- The fort of **San Juan de Ulua,** whose construction began in 1535, was intended to protect the port from pirates. It was later used to (unsuccessfully) defend against the American and French invasions, and it has also served both as a prison and, for a short period, as the residence of Mexico's president. It sits on an island guarding the harbor and now is connected to the mainland by causeway. English-speaking guides can tell you the history of this magnificent fort. It looks like something out of a movie set, only real.

Balloons are a very important part of any plaza celebration. (Photo by Dwight Carlos Hughes)

- **Museo de la Ciudad,** located at Ave. Zaragoza at Morelos, provides a good overview of the city's history, with many interesting artifacts and displays. It even has a scale model of the city that will help you navigate to other sights, should you wish to wander independently. English-speaking students will be readily available to explain everything.
- The **Baluarte de Santiago,** located at Canal at 16 de Septiembre, is the last remaining portion of the original city walls that were once topped by nine forts built by the Spanish. It's well-lit at night and you often see it in tourist brochures of Veracruz. In its massive walls, a small museum displays pre-Columbian gold jewelry.

The beaches in Veracruz are not good and the harbor is polluted. The beach resorts and high rises are located a few miles south of the city. Because it is easy to access from Mexico City, many Mexicans choose to vacation in Veracruz rather than the more popular destinations of foreigners.

If you are fortunate enough to visit Veracruz during *carnaval* (the week prior to Ash Wednesday) you will be in for a real treat! This is one of the most colorful, event-filled **Mardi Gras celebrations** anywhere in the country. You are sure to be caught up in the festivities. However, be forewarned that all hotels are filled well in advance and reservations are a must! Enjoy!

7.4 Veracruz to Tlaxcala

Distance   *345 km (214 mi.)*

Features   *This is a day of mostly high-speed driving on cuota (toll roads), to end up in one of the most delightful small cities in Mexico. It follows the route that Hernan Cortes and his conquistadors used to make their assault on the Aztec nation. Later, tons of gold, silver, and plunder were shipped to Spain via this route.*

Work your way down to the waterfront and head south along a nice beachfront boulevard to the modern beach section of Veracruz with its hotels and resorts. After passing through this area and departing the town, look for signs to Hwy. 150D *cuota* toward Mexico City. This will soon lead you to the *autopista* (expressway) toward Mexico City. Be prepared for a significant change in altitude along this route, as you will climb out of the steamy coast and into the rain forest and mountains ahead. Fog and wet pavement are not unusual.

Many remote haciendas, like this one which dates back to the 1500s, provide wonderful overnight stops.

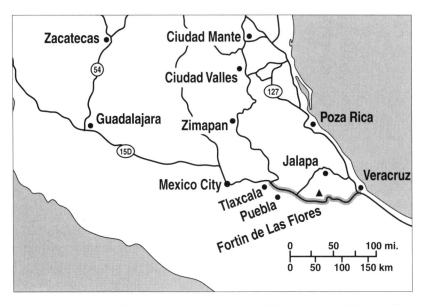

For the rest of the day, just follow signs to Mexico City. About 40 km (25 mi.) after passing **Puebla,** take the exit to Tlaxcala.

Two delightful towns along this route, Cordoba and Fortin de las Flores, are well worth a stop. **Cordoba** is located approximately 135 km (84 mi.) from Veracruz. It sits amid lush vegetation and flowers. The central square and surrounding architecture are right out of Andalucia. The *iglesia parroquial* (parish church) contains a very large bell known as the *Santa Maria.* The **town hall** is also an impressive sight. **Fortin de las Flores** is only four miles further to the west, and you will see why it was named "Little Fortress of Flowers." The residents are very proud of their reputation for beautiful flowers, and you will see orchids, gardenias, azaleas, and many other types everywhere. Many of the tropical flowers sold in the Mexico City markets are grown around here. On a clear day, you may get a view of the 18,700-foot volcano **Pico de Orizaba.**

Upon arriving at **Tlaxcala,** leave the expressway and cross the river bridge. Four blocks later, turn right on Juarez Street and follow the signs to the *centro,* **Plaza de la Constitucion,** only two blocks away. Located right on the plaza is the wonderful **Hotel Posada San Francisco** ($65;

tel. 246-26022; e-mail info@posadafrancisco.com). This old mansion has been renovated into an elegant hotel with all facilities. Secure parking is available nearby and included in the room rate.

Tlaxcala (population 60,000) is the capital city of the state of Tlaxcala. It derives its name from the Indian nation that was here when the Spanish landed. They were bitter enemies of the Aztec and soon allied with the Spanish, adding more than 10,000 men to their 500-man force. Today, Tlaxcala is one of the most beautiful and interesting cities in Mexico. The **Plaza de las Constitucion** is particularly lovely and surrounded by carefully-restored colonial buildings. The interior walls of the **Palacio de Gobierno** (Government Palace) have been painted with more than 450 vivid murals by **Disiderio Hernandez Xochitiotzin** that outline the preconquest life. Although there are no formal tours explaining the paintings, ask around in the various offices, and someone will locate an English-speaking worker who can go into great detail explaining their meaning.

The **Catedral de Nuestra Señora de la Asuncion,** located only one block off this main square, is one of the oldest

Laundry is done a little differently in rural Mexico.

churches in Mexico and it shows an early Moorish influence. An adjoining building that was once a monastery now contains a **small museum** of paintings and other artifacts from this area. **The Plaza de Toros,** located on Calle Capilla Abierta just off Independencia, may be the oldest bullring in Mexico. It is now only used during state fairs, but you can visit it throughout the year. There are several other interesting sites in this town which could make for a pleasant two-night stay.

7.5 Tlaxcala to Zimapan

. . . .

Distance   *280 km (172 mi.)*

Features   *This day offers some magnificent mountain riding through Indian country. The destination is not the city of Zimapan itself, but the world-class Royal Spa on the outskirts of the city.*

After departing the plaza in Tlaxcala, work your way back to Hwy. 117 toward Apizaco. In just a few short miles, the left turn onto Hwy. 136 toward Calpulalpan will be obvious. Please be on the alert, as this can be a very busy stretch of road with lots of truck traffic. Approximately 60 km (42 mi.) after this turn you will arrive in **Calpulalpan.** From here, make a right turn onto Hwy. 130 toward Pachuca for a delightful, twisting, turning ride with magnificent views through the canyons.

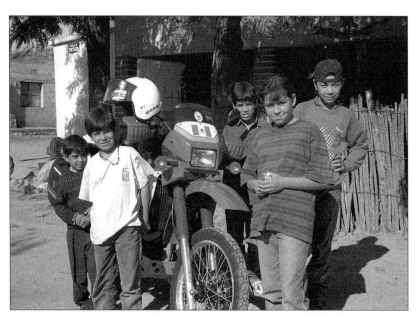

Your arrival in a small Mexican village on a motorcycle is sure to attract a crowd.
(Photo by Judy Kennedy)

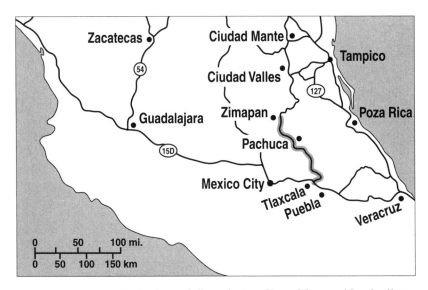

In Pachuca, follow signs to Hwy. 85 toward Ixmiquilpan. **Pachuca,** with more than 200,000 inhabitants, was originally founded as a mining center, and the mines in the area still produce large quantities of silver even today. The hilly landscape surrounding this city is covered with colorful houses that make for wonderful photo opportunities. The city itself has the usual sights, such as the central square, church, and regional museums, but Pachuca's most unique attraction is the **Museo Nacional de Fotografia,** located on the second floor of the former monastery of San Francisco. It contains a good collection of pictures outlining Mexican history from the earliest days of photography to the present. Pachuca is a difficult city to navigate and I would suggest hiring a taxi to guide you through.

From Pachuca, follow Hwy. 85 to Zimapan, only 105 km (65 mi.) away. Stay on Hwy. 85 to bypass the town itself, and just north you will find the **Royal Spa** on your left. The Royal Spa, Carretera Mexico Laredo km 205 ($60; tel. 772-82773), is a great place to pet your body and enjoy yourself. The wonderful hotel and world-class spa are typically frequented by wealthy Mexicans who come for a week or more to revitalize themselves at this oasis in the countryside. By arriving early, you should be able to get a much-needed massage and partake of the rest of their wide array of services.

7.6 Zimapan to Ciudad Valles

Distance   *270 km (168 mi.)*

Features   *This is one of my favorite rides in Mexico. It will lead you through remote jungle before twisting and turning down to the broad coastal plain. There will be very little traffic on this route and the road conditions will be good, but don't let the mileage fool you—hairpins, jungle mountain views, and twisties will make you want to take this at a leisurely pace. The 150 km (94 mi.) from Zimapan to Tamazunchale took me almost three hours the last time I rode this route.*

Native handicrafts make great souvenirs of your trip to Mexico. (Photo by Lavoe Davis)

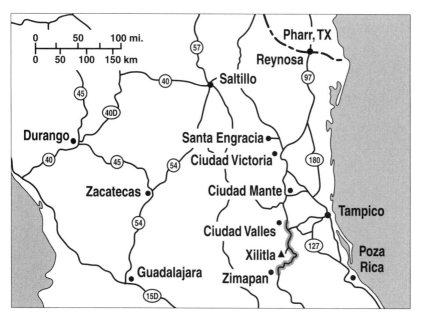

Leaving the hotel, continue north on Hwy. 85, your route for today, which is notable for its having been part of the original **Pan-American Highway.** Just continue on toward Tamazunchale and Ciudad Valles. Enjoy! After Tamazunchale the speed will pick up. **Tamazunchale** (population 65,000) is located in lush jungle surroundings and it was once a major overnight stop on the Pan-American Highway. Today, it is a sleepy little town with adequate services. The **Hotel Tamazunchale** is the best hotel in town, should you want to stay the night.

Side Trip About 35 km (22 mi.) north of Tumazunchale, Hwy. 120 will be clearly marked toward **Xilitla.** One of the strangest spots I have ever visited lies only 22 km (14 mi.) beyond that left turn. As you approach the town, take a right turn onto a dirt road. (If you cross the bridge you have gone too far.) The dirt road was in good condition the last time I was there, and your destination is not far. **Las Pozas** (the pools) and **La Casa de Ingles** (English House) were the home of the late, eccentric millionaire **Edward James,** a friend of artists Dali and Picasso—and his love for their styles of art will soon be evident!

*Edwin James' surreal dream lies decaying in the midst of the
jungle near Xilitla.*

Rumored to be the illegitimate son of **King Edward VII,** James escaped to this remote area and spent more than twenty years building surrealist concrete structures and planning a vast estate. Most of it was never finished and it's all being overtaken by the jungle now. The river that runs through this area has several pools that are popular swimming holes for the local children. Vendors will have their wares spread out on blankets for you to view. Walk the grounds, enjoy the jungle, and try to imagine what must have been going on in this man's mind. After your visit, return to the highway and continue north. ■

As you travel through **Ciudad Valles,** the **Hotel Valles** ($40; tel. 138-2-00-22), located on the right on Hwy. 85 and Blvd. # 36 N is a real treat. When I first stayed here in 1972 it was somewhat threadbare and worn, but it has since been renovated and is now a good value for the money. The lush tropical grounds are a delight. It has secure parking and a good restaurant.

7.7 Ciudad Valles to Santa Engracia

· ·

Distance   *230 km (140 mi.)*

Features   *Expect an easy day riding two-lane road through jungle, cane fields, and citrus orchards. This route retraces portions of the original Pan-American Highway. In most places, the road is narrow and vegetation grows right to the pavement. Your destination is the wonderful Hacienda Santa Engracia.*

After a wonderful, relaxing morning at Hotel Valles, head north through low savannah lands on Hwy. 85 toward Ciudad Mante. Continue on 85 toward Ciudad Victoria. As you approach Ciudad Victoria, follow signs to Monterrey to bypass the main downtown section. This road was in fair condition the last time I traveled it.

About 35 km (22 mi.) after leaving Ciudad Victoria, the left turn to Santa Engracia will be clearly marked. From there, it is 20 km (12 mi.) to the *hacienda* through citrus groves and several small villages. Just follow the pavement. As you approach the village of **Santa Engracia,** the white

The Green Angels truck is one of the most welcome sights you may ever see in Mexico.

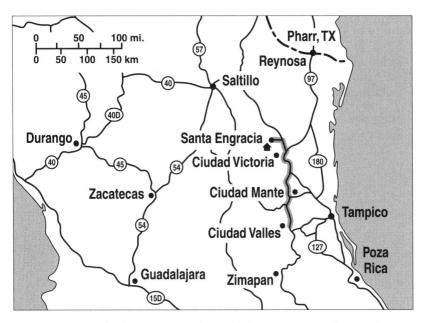

building on your right with large palm trees is your destination. If you reach the end of the pavement, you have gone about 300 yards too far.

Hacienda Santa Engracia ($35; tel. 131-6-10-61) is an absolute "must" overnight stay. The land was given to the family in the 1500s by Spanish land grant and has remained in the family to this day. The *hacienda* itself, once the family home, will give you a real feel for colonial Mexico. The accommodations are modern, but basic. The grounds are lush and peaceful. It has a nice pool and even a tennis court. No need to read a menu here—you'll eat what the family is eating! With only 26 rooms, the hacienda can fill up quickly on weekends; during the week you will probably be the only guest.

7.8 Santa Engracia to Pharr, Texas

Distance   *250 km (155 mi.)*

Features   *Your goal today will be to arrive back in the United States safely. The route retraces part of the route of your first day, leaving plenty of time for you to continue on past the border if you wish.*

Retrace the route from Santa Engracia to the intersection with Hwy. 85. Every map I have seen shows that Hwy. 60 toward Gomez is to the north of this intersection—but this is not correct! Turn right and go 7 km (4 mi.) south and take the clearly-marked left turn. After 12 km (7 mi.) you will reach a T-intersection with no signage. Turn left (north) onto Hwy. 180. From there, follow signs to Reynosa. Upon entering **Reynosa,** follow the signs to the international bridge.

Most Mexican towns are built around a central plaza.

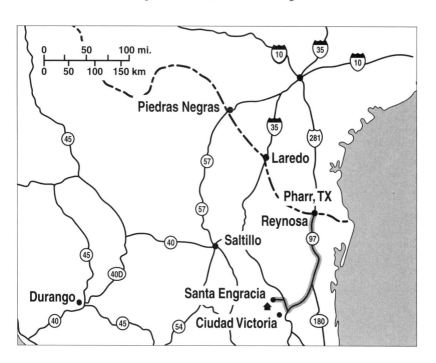

Appendices

A1 A Little Spanish

You can travel in northern Mexico and speak no Spanish, but I don't recommend it since it will make things more difficult and cause frustration. Please spend a few hours with some tapes to pick up a few basic phrases. Not only will this help you directly in your travels, you will likely be rewarded with a friendly smile and assistance for having made an attempt to communicate. Since Spanish pronunciation is very regular, a little time spent familiarizing yourself with the rules can reap big rewards.

Pronunciation

Most letters in Spanish are pronounced very similar to their English counterparts. These few simple rules note some of the general variations. You can practice by applying this guide to other words listed in the text and appendices.

Spanish Letter	English Sound	Example	Pronounced
A	ah (yacht)	*padre*	PAH-dray
E	ay (day)	*español*	ays-pah-NYOHL
I	ee (meet)	*libro*	LEE-broh
O	oh (open)	*moto*	MOH-toh
U	oo (tooth)	*mucho*	MOO-choh
AU	ow (cow)	*auto*	OW-toh
AI	y (type)	*baile*	BYE-lay
IE	yeh (yet)	*abierto*	ah-VYER-toh
UE	weh (wet)	*bueno*	BWEH-noh
C (before a, o, u)	k (cat)	*campo*	KAHM-poh
C (before e, i)	s (cent)	*cinco*	SEEN-koh
G (before a, o, u)	g (go)	*guerra*	GAY-rrah
G (before e, i)	h (hot)	*general*	hay-nay-RAHL
H	silent	*hasta*	AHS-tah
J	h (hot)	*jardín*	hahr-DEEN
LL	y (yes)	*pollo*	POH-yoh
Ñ	ny (canyon)	*señorita*	say-nyohr-REE-tah
QU	k (keep)	*que*	kay
R	roll once	*caro*	KAH-doh
RR	rroll twice	*perro*	PAY-rroh

S	s (see)	*rosa*	ROH-sah
V	b (book)	*primavera*	pree-mah-BAY-rah
X	s (sign)	*examinar*	ays-ahm-mee-NAHR
Z	s (sane)	*zapato*	sah-PAH-toh

Stress and Accents

Spanish also uses very regular rules to apply stress to syllables in a word:

- Words ending in a vowel, N, or S are stressed on the second-to-last syllable.
- Words ending in a consonant other than N or S are stressed on the last syllable.
- Words that are exceptions to the two rules above must have an accent mark over the stressed syllable.

Daily Politeness

Listed below is a basic vocabulary of words and phrases which you can use to practice your pronunciation; consult a good Spanish-English dictionary for less common words. The first two words on the list are the most important.

thank you	*gracias*	GRAH-syahs
please	*por favor*	POR fah-VOHR
you're welcome	*de nada*	DAY NAH-dah
good morning	*buenos días*	BWAY-nos DEE-ahs
good afternoon	*buenas tardes*	BWAY-nahs TAHR-days
good night	*buenas noches*	BWAY-nahs NOH-chays
How are you?	*¿Cómo está?*	COH-moh ays-TAH
I am fine	*Estoy bien*	ays-TOY BYEHN
excuse me	*perdóneme.*	pehr-DOH-nay-may
Goodbye!	*¡Adiós!*	ah-DYOHS
yes	*sí*	SEE
no	*no*	NOH
bad	*malo*	MAH-loh
good	*bueno*	BWAY-noh
more	*más*	MAHS
less	*menos*	MAY-nohs

At the Border

bike title	*título de propiedad*	TEE-too-loh DAY proh-pree-ay-DAD
registration	*registración*	ray-hee-strah-SYOHN
Customs	*Aduana*	ah-DWAH-nah
Immigration	*Immigración*	eem-ee-grah-SYOHN
identification	*identificación*	ee-dayn-tee-fee-cah-SYOHN
passport	*pasaporte*	pah-sah-POHR-tay
tourist card	*tarjeta de turista*	tahr-HAY-tah day too-REE-stah
credit card	*tarjeta de crédito*	tahr-HAY-tah day CRAY-dee-toh
vehicle permit	*permiso de importación*	pehr-MEE-soh DAY eem-pohr-tah-SYOHN
	temporal de vehículo	tehm-pohr-AHL DAY bay-HEE-kyoo-loh

Basic Verbs and Questions

I want . . .	*Quiero . . .*	KYAY-doh
I need . . .	*Necesito . . .*	nay-say-SEE-toh
I have . . .	*Tengo . . .*	TEHN-goh
Do you have . . . ?	*¿Tiene . . . ?*	TYAY-nay
Do you speak English?	*¿Hablan inglés?*	AH-blan een-GLAYS
How much does this cost?	*¿Cuánto cuesta?*	KWAHN-toh KWAY-stah
I don't understand.	*No entiendo.*	NOH ayn-TYEHN-doh
Where is . . . ?	*¿Dónde está . . . ?*	DOHN-day ays-TAH
How far is . . . ?	*¿A qué distancia está . . . ?*	AH KAY dee-STAHN-syah ays-TAH
How long?	*¿Cuánto tiempo?*	KWAN-toh TYEM-poh

On the Road

left	*izquierda*	ees-KYEHR-dah
right	*derecha*	day-RRAY-chah
straight ahead	*derecho*	day-RRAY-choh
highway	*carretera*	kah-rray-TAY-dah
road	*camino*	cah-MEE-noh
street	*calle*	KAH-YAY
north	*norte*	NOHR-tay
south	*sur*	SOOD
east	*este*	AYS-tay
west	*oeste*	oh-AYS-tay
traffic light	*luz*	LOOS
blinking/flashing lights	*luces intermitentes*	LOO-says een-tehr-mee-TAYN-tays
gasoline	*gasolina*	gah-soh-LEE-nah

unleaded	*sin plomo, magna sin*	SEEN PLOH-mo, MAHG-nah SEEN
full	*lleno*	YAY-noh
oil	*aceite*	ah-say-EE-tay
puncture	*agujero*	ah-goo-HAY-doh
front tire/rim	*llanta delanteros*	YAHN-tah day-lan-TAY-dohs
back tire/rim	*llanta delantera trasera*	YAHN-tah day-lan-TAY-dah trah-SAY-dah
inner tube	*tubo interior*	TOO-boh een-tay-RYOHR
air/fuel filter	*filtro de aire/combustible*	FEEL-troh DAY AY-day/cohm-boo-STEE-blay
spark plugs	*bujías*	boo-HEE-ahs
gear box	*caja de cambio*	KAH-hah day KAHM-byoh
final drive	*transmisión*	trahns-mee-SYOHN
drive shaft	*eje transmisor*	AY-hay trans-mee-SOHR
chain	*cadena*	kah-DAY-nah
master link	*eslabón principal*	ays-lah-BOHN preen-see-PAHL
cooling system	*agua del radiador*	AH-gwah dehl rah-dee-ah-DOHR
anti-freeze	*anti-congelante*	AHN-tee cohn-gay-LAHN-tay
nut/bolt	*tornillo*	tohr-NEE-yoh
washer	*arandela*	ah-dahn-DAY-lah
compressed air	*aire a presión*	AY-day ah pray-SYOHN
axle	*eje*	AY-hay
front brakes	*frenos delanteros*	FRAY-nohs day-lan-TAY-dohs
rear brakes	*frenos traseros*	FRAY-nohs trah-SAY-dohs
brake/clutch fluid	*Liquido de freno/embrague*	lee-KWEE-doh day FRAY-noh/aym-BRAH-gay
brake/clutch cable	*Cable de frenos/embrague*	KAH-blay day FRAY-noh/aym-BRAH-gay
fuse	*fusible*	foo-SEE-blay
headlight bulb	*faro delantero*	FAH-doh day-lan-TAY-doh
taillight bulb	*bombilla piloto*	bohm-BEE-yah pee-LOH-toh
dead battery	*batería descargada*	bah-tay-REE-ah days-kahr-GAH-dah
distilled water	*agua destilada*	AH-gwah day-stee-LAH-dah
muffler	*mofle*	MOH-flay
spring	*muelle*	moo-AY-YAY

An octagonal sign always means STOP

STOP

Triangular signs always mean CAUTION

WORKMEN

**TOPES
(SPEED BUMPS)**

**SCHOOL
CROSSING**

Rectangular signs are INFORMATIONAL

NO LEFT TURN

**PARKING
(ESTACIONAMIENTO)**

**ONE HOUR PARKING
(ESTACIONAMIENTO)**

SCHOOL

Highway Signs

These will generally give you no problem, as Mexico uses international symbols.

stop	alto	AHL-toh
keep to right	conserve su derecha	cohn-SEHR-bay soo day-RRAY-chah
dangerous curve	curva peligrosa	KOOHR-bah pay-lee-GROH-sah
no passing	no rebase	NOH ray-BAH-say
school zone	zona escolar	SOHN-ah ays-koh-LAHR
slow down	disminuya su velocidad	dees-mee-NOO-yah soo bay-loh-see-DAHD
danger	peligro	pay-LEE-groh
speed bumps	topes/vibradores	TOH-pays/bee-brah-DOHR-ays
toll route	cuota	KWOH-tah
free route	libre	LEE-bray
detour	desviación	des-vee-ah-SYOHN
men working	hombres trabajando	OHM-brays trah-bah-HAHN-doh
freeway	autopista	ow-toh-PEE-stah

Accommodations

hotel	hotel	oh-TEL
room	habitación	ah-vee-tah-SYOHN
for one person	para una persona	PAH-dah OO-nah pehr-SOH-nah
for two persons	para dos personas	PAH-dah DOHS pehr-SOH-nahs
one bed	sencillo	sen-SEE-yoh
two beds	doble	DOH-blay
with bath	con baño	cohn BAH-nyoh
hot water	agua caliente	AH-gwah kah-lee-AYN-tay
towel	toalla	toh-AH-yah
soap	jabón	ha-BOHN
toilet paper	papel higiénico	pah-PEHL ee-HYAY-nee-koh

Numbers

0	cero	SAY-doh
1	uno, una	OO-noh, OO-nah
2	dos	DOHS
3	tres	TRAYS

4	*cuatro*	KWAH-troh
5	*cinco*	SEEN-koh
6	*seis*	SAYS
7	*siete*	see-AY-tay
8	*ocho*	OH-choh
9	*nueve*	noo-AY-vay
10	*diez*	DYAYS
11	*once*	OHN-say
12	*doce*	DOH-say
13	*trece*	TRAY-say
14	*catorce*	kah-TOHR-say
15	*quince*	KEEN-say
16	*dieciséis*	dee-ay-see-SAYS
17	*diecisiete*	dee-ay-see-see-AY-tay
18	*dieciocho*	dee-ay-see-OH-cho
19	*diecinueve*	dee-ay-see-noo-AY-vay
20	*veinte*	BAYN-tay
21	*veintiuno*	bayn-tee-OO-noh
22	*veintidós*	bayn-tee-DOHS
30	*treinta*	TRAYN-tah
40	*cuarenta*	kwah-DAYN-tah
50	*cincuenta*	seen-KWAYN-tah
60	*sesenta*	say-SAYN-tah
70	*setenta*	say-TAYN-tah
80	*ochenta*	oh-CHAYN-tah
90	*noventa*	noh-BAYN-tah
100	*cien*	SYEN
200	*doscientos*	doh-SYEN-tohs
1000	*mil*	MEEL

A2 On the Menu (la carta)

Tableware

spoon	cuchara	koo-CHAH-dah
knife	cuchillo	koo-CHEE-yoh
plate	plato	PLAH-toh
fork	tenedor	tay-nay-DOHR
cup	taza	TAH-sah
glass	vaso	BAH-soh
napkin	servilleta	sehr-bee-YAY-tah

Drinks (bebidas)

water	agua	AH-gwah
mineral water	agua mineral	AH-gwah mee-nehr-AHL
coffee	café	kah-FAY
coffee with hot milk	café con leche	kah-FAY kohn LAY-chay
coffee with cream	café con crema	kah-FAY kohn KRAY-mah
black coffee	café negro	kah-FAY NAY-groh
soft drinks	refrescos	ray-FRAYS-kohs
fruit juice	jugo	HOO-goh
tea	té	TAY
beer	cerveza	sehr-BAY-sah
red wine	vino rojo	BEE-noh RROH-hoh
white wine	vino blanco	BEE-noh BLAHN-koh

Breakfast (desayuno)

bread	pan	PAHN
toast	pan tostado	PAHN tohs-TAH-doh
butter	mantequilla	man-tay-KEE-yah
jelly	mermelada	mehr-may-LAH-dah
eggs	huevos	hoo-AY-vohs
scrambled eggs	huevos revueltos	hoo-AY-vohs ray-VWAYL-tohs
fried/sunny-side up eggs	huevos fritos	hoo-AY-vohs FREE-tohs
eggs scrambled with chiles, onions, and tomatoes	huevos mexicanos	hoo-AY-vohs may-hee-KAHN-ohs

fried eggs covered with salsa	*huevos rancheros*	hoo-AY-vohs rrahn-CHAY-dos
sweet rolls	*pan dulce*	pahn DOOL-say
bacon	*tocino*	toh-SEE-noh
ham	*jamón*	hah-MOHN

Meats and Poultry

chicken	*pollo*	POH-yoh
chicken breast	*pechuga*	pay-CHOO-gah
turkey	*pavo*	PAH-boh
duck	*pato*	PAH-toh
meat	*carne*	KAHR-nay
beef	*res*	RAYS
beefsteak	*bistec*	BEES-tayk
hamburger	*hamburguesa*	ahm-boor-GAY-sah
pork	*puerco*	PWEHR-koh
pork sausage (hot)	*chorizo*	choh-DEE-soh
pork rinds	*chicharrón*	chee-chah-RROHN
goat	*cabra*	KAH-brah
young goat	*cabrito*	kah-BREE-toh
veal	*ternera*	tay-NAY-dah

Seafood

fish	*pescado*	pays-KAH-doh
filet	*filete de pescado*	fee-LAY-tay day pays-KAH-doh
fried whole fish	*frito pescado*	FREE-toh pays-KAH-doh
fried filet of fish	*filete de pescado frito*	fee-LAY-tay day pays-KAH-doh FREE-toh
tuna	*atún*	ah-TOON
bass	*corvina*	kohr-BEE-nah
red snapper	*huachinango*	wah-chee-NAHN-goh
salmon	*salmón*	sal-MOHN
shark	*tiburón*	tee-boo-DOHN
trout	*trucha*	TROO-chah
lobster	*langosta*	lahn-GOH-stah
snail	*caracol*	kah-dah-COHL
clams	*almejas*	ahl-MAY-hahs
squid	*calamar*	kah-lah-MAHR
shrimp	*camarones*	kah-mah-RROH-nays

Fruits

orange	*naranja*	nah-DAHN-hah
apple	*manzana*	mahn-SAHN-ah
lime	*limón*	lee-MOHN
mango	*mango*	MAHN-goh
grape	*uva*	OO-bah
grapefruit	*toronja*	toh-DOHN-hah

Preparation

grilled over charcoal	*al carbón*	ahl kahr-BOHN
grilled	*asada*	ah-SAH-dah
boiled	*cocido*	koh-SEE-doh
breaded, Italian-style	*milanesa*	mee-lah-NAY-sah
fried	*frito*	FREE-toh
rare	*poco cocido*	POH-koh koh-SEE-doh
well done	*bien cocido*	BYEHN koh-SEE-doh
smoked	*ahumado*	ah-oo-MAH-doh
baked	*al horno*	ahl OHR-noh
fried in butter and garlic	*al mojo de ajo*	ahl MOH-hoh day AH-hoh
broiled or baked and covered in a tomato sauce with olives	*veracruz*	bay-dah-KROOS

Vegetables

tomato	*tomate*	toh-MAH-tay
onion	*cebolla*	say-BOH-lah
mushrooms	*champiñones*	chahm-pee-NYOH-nays
carrot	*zanahoria*	sah-nah-oh-DEE-ah
radish	*rábano*	RRAH-bah-noh
potatoes	*papas*	PAH-pahs
beans	*frijoles*	free-HOH-lays
asparagus	*espàrragos*	ays-PAH-rrah-gos
avocado	*aquacate*	ah-kwah-KAH-tay
lettuce	*lechuga*	lay-CHOO-gah
garlic	*ajo*	AH-hoh

Mexican Specialties

tortilla	presented with almost every meal, these can be made thick or thin, from corn, wheat, or flour

enchilada	combinations of meat, chicken, or seafood with beans, cheese, salsa, or chili, rolled in a *tortilla,* then baked
burrito	same as an *enchilada* but wrapped in a wheat or flour *tortilla*
torta	sandwich on a roll
taco	same as an *enchilada* or *burrito,* but wrapped in a soft corn *tortilla*
chiles rellenos	deep-fried chilies stuffed with cheese
guacamole	mashed avocado mixed with onion, tomato, chili, and lemon, served cold
quesadilla	a flour *tortilla* topped with cheese, then baked
tamal	corn dough stuffed with combinations of meat, cheeses, and beans, wrapped and steamed in corn husks
sincronizada	grilled ham and cheese sandwich

Sweets

ice cream	*helado*	ay-LAH-doh
cream caramel	*flan*	FLAHN
crepe	*crepa*	KRAY-pah
pastry	*pastel*	pahs-TAYL

A3 Packing List

●●

Packing for a trip in Mexico is not much different than packing for the same trip in the U.S. Consider the expected weather conditions and your personal preferences. Since most of the routes in this book have dramatic changes in altitude, conditions can vary greatly from day to day. In addition to your regular gear, I also suggest you carry:

- Tire repair kit
- Shop manual
- Master link for your drive chain
- Parts that are prone to breaking on your particular model of bike
- Spare sunglasses and prescription glasses
- Washcloth
- Spanish-English dictionary or translator
- Water bottle
- Hand cleaner/hand wipes
- A supply of spare prescription medications kept in a different place than the supply you plan to use
- Ear plugs
- Small flashlight for your bedside

A4 Other References

••

This book has all the information you need to know to ride in Mexico. However, I recommend you read and carry some of the following with you to increase your enjoyment of the trip.

Before you go, your best source for learning about the habits and customs of Mexico is Carl Franz's *The People's Guide to Mexico* (John Muir Publications). Also, Joe Cummings' *Northern Mexico Handbook* (Moon Publications) covers portions of this area in great detail. If you want to know more history and culture, this is the book for you. Also, *Mexico* in the Lonely Planet series (Lonely Planet Publications) offers many more hotel and restaurant choices than I have listed. The American Automobile Association's *Mexico TravelBook* can be a great source for locating an acceptable hotel at the end of the day. However, it does not include lodgings in many of the smaller towns.

The most detailed maps of Mexico that I have ever seen are found in PEMEX's *Atlas de Carreteras y Ciudades (Road Atlas and Tourist Cities),* a 70-page paperback booklet sponsored by the Mexican fuel company and distributed by the Ministry of Tourism of Mexico. Unfortunately, the most recent edition (the 2nd) is now out of print. If, by chance, you can get your hands on a copy, buy it—and guard it with your life! You will find passable back roads here that are not identified on any of the more popular maps of the country.

Kummerly + Frey, the well-known European mapmaker, also has several good maps of Mexico which can be ordered through the publisher of this book, Whitehorse Press (800-531-1133). I have also used and liked the maps furnished by both the American Automobile Association and Sanborn's (the specialist for Mexican insurance), but the PEMEX maps mentioned above are the best. I hope that another edition of this valuable atlas will be published in the near future.

A5 Tours & Rentals

Many options exist if you don't want to ride alone or aren't able to bring your own motorcycle south. Pancho Villa Moto-Tours, a company founded in 1981 by Skip Mascorro, is credited by many with "opening" Mexico to two-wheeled travel—one could always travel there by motorcycle, of course, but Skip made such trips practical by taking care of the endless details so his riders could focus on the thrill of the ride and Mexico's natural beauty, history, and rich culture. PVMT rents bikes for self-touring and also leads guided tours (both street and dual-sport) to the areas discussed in this book, as well as many other places of interest in Central and South America. If you want to "Ride With A Legend," contact Skip or his wife, Nancy, for current schedules and prices at:

Pancho Villa Moto-Tours (Skip Mascorro)
4510 Highway 281 North #3
Spring Branch, TX 78070
800-233-0564 (toll free)
830-438-7744 (phone)
830-438-7745 (fax)
www.panchovilla.com
info@panchovilla.com

Experts in touring the Americas and other exotic destinations.

Other groups offering tours and rentals (at the time of the first printing of this book) are worth a check as well, although I do not have firsthand experience with the companies listed below.

Edelweiss Bike Travel (Werner Wachter)
Sport-Platzweg 14
A-64-14 Unter-Mieming

Austria
Represented in U.S. by Tri-Community Travel
800-582-2263 (toll free)
619-249-5825 (phone)
Austrian home office phone +43-5264-5690
Worldwide fax +43-5264-58533
www.edelweissbiketravel.com
edelweiss@tirol.com

Well-known as one of the premier motorcycle touring companies worldwide.

Mototour Mexico (Ricardo Barbosa)
Morelos 212-A
Santa Maria Ahuacatitlan
Cuernavaca, Morelos 62100
Mexico
Represented in U.S. by Ponderosa Travel (Hilda)
800-229-3633 (toll free)
Mexican home office phone 52-73-130-732
Worldwide fax 52-73-133-575
Http://central.edsa.net.mx/mototourmexico
ponderosatvl@earthlink.net

Offer central and southern Mexico "budget" tours—budget prices, quality tours.

Rosen's Rides, Inc. (Dan Rosen)
1135 Terminal Way #209
Reno, NV 89502
800-484-9250 X5409 (toll free)
512-480-9967 (phone)
www.rosensrides.com
info@rosensrides.com

Specialists for Mexico's Copper Canyon and the Sierra Madre Range.

Tex-Mex Moto Tours Inc. (Herbert Gabler)
1108 Tyra Lane
Fort Worth, TX   76114
817-626-7567 (phone)
817-336-1312 (fax)
www.texmextours.net

Street, off-road, and sidecar tours available

A6 Transport Services

....

If you have limited time available, consider shipping your motorcycle to the border and flying down to meet it, so you can maximize the amount of time you spend in Mexico. This can be an especially attractive option for riders living above the Mason-Dixon line. A number of brokers have partnered with the major U.S. moving companies to specialize in no-fuss motorcycle transport.

Count on spending between fifteen and twenty cents per mile (as the crow flies) to ship your bike, and allow at least two weeks for delivery to the mover's terminal at any major southern U.S. airport. You can arrange for the bike to be picked up at your home or office. Most of the transport companies use special motorcycle-appropriate skids with pads and tie-downs (no crating necessary), all designed to deliver your bike in mint condition. Insurance is also available at affordable rates. You will be amazed at how easy and efficient these services make the whole process. For a free estimate and detailed information, call any of the brokers listed below.

Federal/Allied Transport (Rhonda Nagel)
101 National Road
East Peoria, IL 61611
800-747-4100, Ext. 222 (toll free)

Federal ships close to 800 motorcycles per month and also handled all of the motorcycles for the traveling Guggenheim exhibit, so they have plenty of experience.

Liberty/Allied Transport (Bud Kindermann)
17 Central Avenue
Hauppaue, NY 11788
800-640-4487, Ext. 1 (pricing info) or Ext. 228 (Bud)

*Bud is the special American Motorcycle Association rep at
Liberty, and he has been extremely helpful to me on a number
of occasions.*

J.C. Motors/North American Van Lines

1260 Logan Avenue A-8
Costa Mesa, CA 92626
714-557-2558 (phone)
www.jcmotors.com
shipping@jcmotors.com

*A new service brokered by one of the larger California
dealers.*

A7 Fiestas and Events

● ●

It seems as if there is always a festival in Mexico. Every town honors its patron saint at some point during the year, usually with fireworks, parades, colorful attire, and public parties. But almost any occasion can be a good excuse to get together and have a good time—and *norteamericanos* are more than welcome. Here are a few of the better-known holidays, plus some motorcycle events. If you plan to be in the country at any of these times, try to take them in. You'll have a wonderful time and make many new friends. On holidays and on Sundays, expect banks and public buildings to be closed.

January	1	Año Nuevo (New Year's Day)
	6	Dia de los Santos Reyes (Three Kings Day)
February	5	Dia de la Constitucion (Constitution Day)
	24	Dia de la Bandera (Flag Day)

Guadalahara has an annual motorcycle rally early in February. The third largest Carnaval in the world (after Rio and New Orleans) is held in Mazatlan each year in late February or early March. Book a hotel early if you want to attend. Veracruz also holds a wonderful Carnaval festival.

March	21	Natalicio Benito Juarez/Primavera (Birthday of President Juarez)

Holy Week and Easter are very special times for Mexicans, with candelit processions and Passion Plays in all major cities.

April *Motorcycle Week in Mazatlan (late April, early May) is one of the largest gatherings of riders in the country.*

May	1	Dia del Trabajo (Labor Day)

5   Cinco de Mayo (Battle of Puebla)

September   1   Opening of Congress and the President's State of the Union Address

16   Dia de la Independencia (Independence Day)

Durango hopes to make their mid-September motorcycle rally an annual event.

October   12   Dia de la Raza (Columbus Day)

A Harley rally is often held in Queretaro in mid-October. Guanajuato holds Mexico's biggest arts festival, the Cervantes Festival (Cervantino), this month.

November   1-2   Dias de los Muertos (Days of the Dead)

20   Dia de la Revolucion (Anniversary of the Revolution)

December   12   Fiesta de Nuestra Señora de Guadalupe (Day of the Virgin of Guadalupe)

25   Navidad (Christmas)

Index

About the Author

Neal Davis was bitten by a travel bug early in life and has spent his years seeking a cure all over the world. As an accomplished sailor and pilot, Davis was also able to ensure that his wife and two children were infected as well, and together they shared many adventures on land, sea, and air. In fact, Davis first got his start motorcycling off-pavement when his young family was taken with the sport.

Years later, when he had retired from owning a small business, Davis took to the street on an organized motorcycle tour of the Alps—and he quickly saw the appeal of two-wheeled travel. Since then, Davis has ridden in 21 countries in nearly every corner of the globe. Over the years, he has also served in various leadership capacities to introduce other motorcyclists to organized touring in Europe and Mexico.

Davis now spends nearly 200 days of every year on the road, living the life we all dream about. Although he has been a long-standing fan of Mexico since the early 70s, he still rode more than 18,000 miles South of the Border in the last year in preparation for this book, most of them on a Kawasaki KLR 650. His favorite street bike, a Honda VFR, currently resides beside his wife's BMW R1100 at their home in Tuscaloosa, Alabama.